BLACKBEARD BUCCANEER

Ralph D. Paine

[ZHINGOORA BOOKS]

This edition is published by
Zhingoora Books.

The Cover is Designed by Pallav Sethiya.

zhingoora_books@yahoo.com

Contents

ILLUSTRATIONS

This Lean, Straight Rover Looked the Part of a Competent Soldier

The Brawn of These Lads Made the Pike a Match for a Pirate's Cutlass

The First Mate Leaped Up with a Horrible Yell

Jack Almost Bumped into the Dugout Canoe

They Capered and Hugged Each Other

He Loomed Like the Belial Whom He Was So Fond of Claiming as His Mentor

CHAPTER I

THAT COURTEOUS PIRATE, CAPTAIN BONNET

THE year of 1718 seems very dim and far away, but the tall lad who sauntered down to the harbor of Charles Town, South Carolina, on a fine, bright morning, was much like the youngsters of this generation. His clothes were quite different, it is true, and he lived in a queer, rough world, but he detested grammar and arithmetic and loved adventure, and would have made a sturdy tackle for a modern high-school football team. He wore a peaked straw hat of Indian weave, a linen shirt open at the throat, short breeches with silver buckles at the knees, and a flint-lock pistol hung from his leather belt.

He passed by scattered houses and stores which were mere log huts loopholed for defense, with shutters and doors of hewn plank heavy enough to stop a musket ball. The unpaved lanes wandered between mud holes in which pigs wallowed enjoyably. Negro slaves, half-naked and bearing heavy burdens, jabbered the dialects of the African jungle from which they had been kidnapped a few months before. Yemassee Indians clad in tanned deer-skins bartered with the merchants and hid their hatred of the English. Jovial, hard-riding gentlemen galloped in from the indigo plantations and dismounted at the tavern to drink and gamble and fight duels at the smallest excuse.

Young Jack Cockrell paid scant heed to these accustomed sights but walked as far as the wharf built of palmetto piling. The wide harbor and the sea that flashed beyond the outer bar were ruffled by a piping breeze out of the northeast. The only vessel at anchor was a heavily sparred brig whose bulwarks were high enough to hide the rows of cannon behind the closed ports.

The lad gazed at the shapely brig with a lively curiosity, as if here was something really interesting. Presently a boat splashed into the water and was tied alongside the vessel while a dozen of the crew tumbled in to sprawl upon the thwarts and shove the oars into the thole-pins. An erect, graceful man in a red coat and a great beaver hat roared a command from the stern-sheets and the pinnace pulled in the direction of the wharf.

"Pirates, to be sure!" said Jack Cockrell to himself, without a sign of alarm. "'Tis Captain Stede Bonnet and his *Royal James*. I know the ship. I saw her when she came in leaking last October and was careened on the beach at Sullivan's Island. A rich voyage this time, for the brig rides deep."

The coast of South Carolina swarmed with pirates two hundred years ago, and they cared not a rap for the law. Indeed, some of these rascals lived on friendly terms with the people of the small settlements and swaggered ashore to squander the broad gold pieces and merchandise stolen from honest trading vessels. You must not blame the South Carolina colonists too harshly because they sometimes welcomed the visiting pirates instead of clapping them in jail. Charles Town was a village at the edge of a wilderness filled with hostile Indians. By sea it stood in fear of attack by the Spaniards of Florida and Havana. There were almost no crops for food and among the population were many runaways from England, loafers and vagabonds who hated the sight of work.

The pirates helped them fight their enemies and did a thriving trade in goods that were sorely needed. Respectable citizens grumbled and one high official was removed in disgrace because he encouraged the pirates to make Charles Town their headquarters, but there was no general outcry unless the sea-rovers happened to molest English ships outside the harbor.

It was Captain Stede Bonnet himself who steered the pinnace and cursed his sweating sailors in a deep voice which went echoing across the bay. He made a brave figure in his scarlet coat, with the brass guard of his naked cutlass winking in the sun. His boat's crew had been mustered from many climes and races, several strapping Englishmen, a wiry, spluttering little Frenchman, a swarthy Portuguese with gold rings in his ears, a brace of stolid Norwegians, and two or three coal black negroes from Barbadoes.

They were well armed, every weapon burnished clean of rust and ready for instant use. Some wore tarnished, sea-stained finery looted from hapless prizes, a brocaded waistcoat, a pair of tasseled jack-boots, a plumed hat, a ruffled cape. The heads of several were bound around with knotted kerchiefs on which dark stains showed,—marks of a brawl aboard the brig or a fight with another ship.

Soon a second boat moved away from the *Royal James* and many people drifted toward the wharf to see the pirates come ashore, but they left plenty of room when the captain scrambled up the weedy ladder and told his men to follow him. Charles Town felt little dread of Stede Bonnet himself. He knew how to conduct himself as a gentleman and the story was well known,—how he had been a major in the British army and a man of wealth and refinement. He had left his home in Barbadoes to follow the trade of piracy because he couldn't get along with his wife, so the rumor ran. At any rate, he seemed oddly out of place among the dirty rogues who sailed under the black flag.

He looked more the soldier than the sailor as he strode along the wharf, his lean, dark visage both grim and melancholy, his chin clean shaven, his mustachios carefully cropped. There were respectful greetings from the crowd of idlers and a gray-haired seaman all warped with rheumatism spoke up louder than the rest.

"Good morrow to ye, Cap'n Bonnet! I be old Sam Griscom that sailed bos'n with you on a marchant voyage out of Liverpool. An' now you are a fine gentleman of fortune, with moidores and pieces of eight to fling at the gals, an' here I be, a sheer hulk on the beach."

Captain Stede Bonnet halted, stared from beneath heavy brows, and a smile made his seamed, sun-dried face almost gentle as he replied:

"It cheers me to run athwart a true old shipmate. A slant of ill fortune, eh, Sam Griscom? You are too old and crippled to sail in the *Royal James*. Here, and a blessing with the gift."

The pirate skipper rammed a hand in his pocket and lung a shower of gold coins at the derelict seaman while the crowd cheered the generous deed. It was easy to guess why Stede Bonnet was something of a hero in Charles Town. He passed on and turned into the street. Most of his ruffians were at his heels but one of the younger of them delayed to pay his compliments to a pretty girl whose manner was sweet and shy and gentle. She had remained aloof from the crowd, having some errand of her own at the wharf, and evidently hoped to be unobserved. Jack Cockrell had failed to notice her, absorbed as he was in gazing his fill of Captain Stede Bonnet.

The girl resented the young pirate's gallantry and would have fled, but he nimbly blocked her path. Just then Jack Cockrell happened to glance that way and his anger flamed hot. He was about to run after Captain Bonnet and beg him to interfere but the maid's distress was too urgent. Her blackguardly admirer was trying to slip his arm around her trim waist while he laughingly demanded a kiss from those fair lips. She evaded him and screamed for help.

There were lusty townsmen among those who beheld the scene but they sheepishly stood in their tracks and were afraid to punish the insolent pirate with his dirk and pistols. He was much taller and heavier than Jack Cockrell, the lad of seventeen, who came of gentlefolk and was unused to brawls with weapons. But the youngster hesitated no more than an instant, although his own pistol lacked a flint and was carried for show.

His quick eye spied a capstan bar which he snatched up as a cudgel. Chivalry had taught him that a man should never reckon the odds when a woman appealed for succor. With a headlong rush he crossed the wharf and swung the hickory bar. The pirate dodged the blow and whipped out his dirk which slithered through Jack's shirt and scratched his shoulder. Undismayed, he aimed a smashing blow at the pirate's wrist and the dirk went spinning into the water.

The rascal tugged at a pistol in his belt but it was awkward work with his left hand and he was bewildered by this amazing attack. Before he could clear for action, Jack smote him on the pate and the battle ended then and there, for the pirate staggered back, missed his footing, and toppled overboard with a tremendous splash.

Leaping to the edge of the wharf, Jack saw him bob to the surface and strike out for shore. Then the doughty young champion ran to offer his escort to the damsel in distress. But she had hastened to slip away from this hateful notoriety and he saw her at the bend of the street where she turned to wave him a grateful farewell.

He would have hastened to overtake her but just then Captain Stede Bonnet came striding back in a temper so black that it terrified his own men. His wrath was not aimed at Jack Cockrell, for he laid a hand upon the lad's arm and exclaimed:

"A shrewd stroke, boy, and a mettlesome spirit! You struck him swift and hard. 'Twould please me better if you had killed the dog."

Stede Bonnet waited with folded arms until the culprit had emerged from the water. Jack Cockrell had punished him severely and there was no more fight in him. His head was reeling, the blood ran into his eyes, and he had swallowed much salt water. Captain Bonnet crooked a finger at him and he obeyed without a word. For a moment they stood face to face, the wretched offender trembling, the captain scowling as he said:

"And so you mistook a lady for a common serving wench, Will Brant? Would ye have Charles Town rise and reeve the ropes about our necks? Is this your promise of good behavior? Learn a lesson then, poor fool."

With the steel-shod butt of a pistol Stede Bonnet hit him squarely between the eyes. He dropped without a groan and lay stretched out as if dead. The captain kicked him once and carelessly shouted:

"Ho, men! Toss this squire o' dames into the pinnace to await our return. And harkee, take warning."

Jack Cockrell felt almost sorry for his fallen foeman but the other pirates grinned and did as they were told. It was a trifling episode. Resuming his stroll to the tavern, Captain Bonnet linked Jack's arm in his and fairly towed him along while the assorted scoundrels trooped behind them. It was shocking company for a lad of the most respectable connections but he felt greatly flattered by the distinction. The name of Stede Bonnet had spread terror from the Capes of the Chesapeake to the blue waters of the Caribbean.

"And so you were unafraid of this bullying Will Brant of mine," said the captain, with one of his pleasant smiles. "You clipped his comb right handsomely. And who may ye be, my brave young sprig?"

"I am John Spencer Cockrell, may it please you, sir," was the answer. "'Twas a small thing to do for a lady. Your pirate would have been too much for me in a fair set-to."

"Pirate? A poor word!" objected Captain Bonnet, his accents severe but the bold eyes twinkling. "We are loyal servants of the King, sworn to do mischief to his lawful enemies,—to wit, all ships and sailors of Spain. For such a young gentleman adventurer as you, Master Cockrell, there is a berth in the *Royal James*. Will ye rendezvous at the tavern and sign your fist to the articles?"

Jack stammered that his kinfolk would never consent, at which Captain Bonnet forbore to coax him but kept a grip on his arm as though they were chums who could not bear to be parted. Down the middle of the street paraded this extraordinary company, the seamen breaking into a song which ran:

> "In Bristowe I left Poll ashore,
> Well stored wi' togs an' gold,

And off I go to sea for more,
A-piratin' so bold.
An' wounded in the arm I got,
An' then a pretty blow;
Comed home I find Poll's flowed away,
Yo, ho, with the rum below!'

Charles Town might be glad to get the pirates' gold but it seemed a timorous welcome, for the merchants peered from their doorways like rabbits when the hounds are loose, and nervous old gentlemen took cover in the near-by alleys. Stede Bonnet knew how to keep his men in hand and allowed only part of the company ashore at once. They were like hilarious children out for a lark, capering outside the tavern to the music of a strolling fiddler or buying horses on the spot and trying to ride them. When they were pitched off on their heads the mirth was uproarious.

In a field beside the tavern some townsmen were shooting at a mark for a prize of a dressed bullock while a group of gentlemen from the plantations were intent on a cock-fight in the tap-room. Here was rare pastime for the frolicsome blades of the *Royal James* and soon they were banging away with their pistols or betting their gold-pieces on the steel-gaffed birds, singing the louder as the bottle was passed. Captain Stede Bonnet stayed prudently sober, ready for any emergency, his demeanor cool and watchful while he chatted with old acquaintances.

He talked often with Jack Cockrell to whom he had taken a strong fancy, and pressed the lad to dine with him. Jack was uneasy at being seen so publicly with a notorious pirate but the experience was delightful beyond words. The captain asked him many questions, twisting his mustachios and staring down from his commanding height with an air of friendly interest. He had found a lad after his own heart.

The seamen tired of their sport and sought new diversion. Some of them kicked off their boots and clinched in wrestling matches for prodigal stakes of gold and jewels. Others found girls to dance with them or wandered off to buy useless trinkets in the shops. Jack Cockrell knew he ought to be posting home to dinner but he was tempted to accept Stede Bonnet's cordial bidding. Boyish friends of his hovered near and regarded him as a hero. No pirate captain had ever deigned to notice them.

Alas for Jack and his puffed-up pride which was doomed to a sudden fall! There advanced from a better quarter of the town a florid, foppishly dressed gentleman of middle age who walked with a pompous gait. He was stout-bodied and the heat of the day oppressed him. Mopping his face with a lace handkerchief or fanning himself with his hat, he halted now and then in a shady spot. Very mindful of his rank and dignit was Mr. Peter Arbuthnot Forbes, sometime London barrister, at present Secretary to the Council of the Province. his own nephew and ward, Jack Cockrell, in this shameful company of roisterers. The august uncle blinked, opened his mouth, and turned as red as a lobster. Indignation choked his speech. For his part, Jack stood dumfounded and quaking, the picture of a coward with a guilty conscience. He would have tried to steal from sight but it was too late.

Captain Stede Bonnet enjoyed the tableau and several of his wicked sailors were mimicking the pompous strut of Mr. Peter Arbuthnot Forbes. Poor Jack mumbled some explanation but his irate uncle first paid his respects to Captain Bonnet.

"Shame to you, sirrah," he cried in a voice that shook with passion. "A man of good birth, by all accounts, who has fallen so low as to lead these vile gallows-birds! And you would entice this lad of mine to follow your dirty trade?"

Captain Bonnet doffed the great beaver hat and bowed low in mocking courtesy. He perceived that this fussy lawyer was not wholly a popinjay, for it required courage to insult a pirate to his face. The reply was therefore milder than expectedd

"Mayhap I am painted blacker than the fact, Councilor. As for this fine stripling who has so disgraced himself, the fault is mine. He risked his life to save a maid from harm. The deed won my affection."

"The maids of Charles Town would need to fear no harm if more pirates were hanged, Captain Bonnet," roundly declared Mr. Forbes, shaking his gold-tipped cane at the freebooter.

"'Tis fortunate for me that you lack the power, my fat and petulant gentleman," was the smiling response.

"Laugh while you may," quoth the other. "These Provinces may soon proclaim joint action against such pests as you."

With a shrug, the Secretary turned to his crestfallen nephew and sharply exclaimed:

"Home with you, John Cockrell. You shall go dinnerless and be locked in your room."

The seamen guffawed at this and Jack furiously resented their ridicule. He was on the point of rebellion as he hotly retorted:

"I am no child to be treated thus, Uncle Peter. Didn't you hear Captain Bonnet report that I had proved myself a man? I trounced one of his own crew, a six-foot bully with a dirk and pistols."

"A fig for that," rapped out Uncle Peter. "Your bully was drunk and helpless, I have no doubt. Will you bandy words with me?"

With this his plump fingers closed on Jack's elbow[20] which he used as a handle to lead him firmly and rapidly away. Behind them pranced a limber young negro who showed every tooth in his head. Jack heard the derisive laughter of the pirates who had hailed him as a hero. His cup of bitterness overflowed when it occurred to him that Captain Bonnet would despise a lad who could be led home in custody of a dandified tyrant of an uncle.

CHAPTER II

THE MERCHANT TRADER, *PLYMOUTH ADVENTURE*

RUBBING his ear which Mr. Peter Arbuthnot Forbes had soundly boxed before releasing him, Jack marched along in gloomy silence until he was conducted into his small, unplastered room. His uncle stalked out and shot the ponderous bolt behind him. Passing through the kitchen, he halted to scold the black cook as a lazy slattern and then sat himself down to a lonely meal. Jack was a problem which the finicky, middle-aged bachelor had been unable to solve. He had undertaken the care of the boy after his parents had died in the same week of a mysterious fever which ravaged the settlement. The uncle failed to realize how fast this strapping youngster was growing into manhood.

He disliked punishing him and was usually unhappy after one of these stormy episodes.

Mr. Peter Forbes pecked at his dinner with little appetite and his plump face was clouded. Shoving back his chair, he paced the floor in a fidgety manner and, at length, opened the door of Jack's room. The hungry prisoner was lounging upon a wooden settle, his chin in his hand, while he sullenly stared at the wall. Always mindful of his manners, he slowly rose to his feet and waited for another scolding.

"I wish we might avoid such scenes as these, Jack," sadly observed Uncle Peter, his hot temper cooled. "No sooner do you leave my sight than some new mischief is afoot."

"You do not understand, sir," impatiently protested the nephew. "In your eyes I am still the urchin who came out from England clinging to his dear mother's skirts. Would ye have me pass my time with girls or have no other friends than snuffy old Parson Throckmorton, my tutor, who tries to pound the Greek and Latin into my thick skull?"

"He is a wise and ripened scholar who wastes his effort," was the dry comment. "Most of the lads of the town are coarse louts who pattern after their ribald elders, Jack. They will lead you into evil courses."

"I shall always pray God to be a gentleman, sir," was the spirited response, "but I must learn to fight my own battles. Were it not for hardy pastimes with these other stout lads, think you I could have cracked the crown of a six-foot pirate?"

Uncle Peter gazed at the boy before he spoke. Tanned and hard and muscular, this was a nephew to be proud of, a man in deeds if not in years, and there was unswerving honesty in the straight mouth and firm chin. The guardian sighed and then annoyance got the better of his affection as he burst out:

"Perdition take all pirates! You were cozened by this hell-rake of a Stede Bonnet and thought it a rare pleasure! John Spencer Cockrell, own nephew to the Secretary of the Colony!"

"I did but copy older men of fair repute," demurely answered Jack, a twinkle in his eye. "Graybeards of Parson Throckmorton's flock traffick in merchandise with the pirates and are mighty civil to them, I note."

"A vile business!" cried Uncle Peter. "It was decided at the recent conference in Virginia that I should go to England as a delegate to lay before His Majesty's Government such evidence as might invoke aid in our campaign against the pirates. It was my intention to leave you in care of Parson Throckmorton, Jack, but I have now resolved to take you with me. And you will remain at school in England. No more of this boon comradeship with villains like Stede Bonnet."

Poor Jack looked most unhappy at the tidings. It was not at all in accord with his ambitions. Here was worse punishment than he had dreamed his uncle could inflict. Dolefully he exclaimed:

"To live in tame and stupid England, locked up in a school? Why, I am big enough to join the forays against the Indians, or to fight bloody battles against the pirates if you really mean to chastise them. But I cannot promise to attack Captain Bonnet. He is a friend of mine."

"You shall come to see him hanged," shouted Mr. Peter Arbuthnot Forbes, very red in the face. "The merchant ship *Plymouth Adventure* is expected soon, and you and I shall take passage in her for Merry

England, thanking heaven to see the last of the barbarous Carolinas for a time."

"Thank your own thanks, sir," grumbled Jack. "Captain Bonnet may be a pirate but he is not nearly so heartless as my own uncle. He asked me to dinner at the tavern. I am faint for lack of food. My stomach sticks to my ribs. 'Tis a great pity you were never a growing boy yourself. For a platter of cold meat and bread I will take my oath to chop you a pile of firewood as high as the kitchen."

The gaoler relented and bustled out to ransack the pantry. Having demolished a joint and a loaf, young John Spencer Cockrell was in a mood much less melancholy. In fact, when he swung the axe behind the fence of hewn palings, he was humming the refrain of that wicked ditty: "*Yo, Ho, with the Rum Below!*" He was tremendously sorry that he had been snatched away from the engaging society of Captain Bonnet and his wild crew, and the future had a gloomy aspect, but even these grievances were forgotten when he descried, in a lane which led past the house, the lovely maid whose cause he had championed at the wharf.

She was Dorothy, only daughter of Colonel Malcolm Stuart who commanded the militia forces of the Colony. Although she was the elder by two or three years and gave herself the airs of a young lady, Jack Cockrell hopelessly, secretly adored her. It was an anti-climax for a hero to be serving out his sentence at the wood-pile and he turned his back to the gate while he made the chips fly. But Dorothy had no intention of ignoring him. She paused with a smile so winsome that Jack's heart fluttered and he dropped the axe to grasp her outstretched hand. He squeezed it so hard that Dorothy winced as she said:

"What a masterful man it is, but please don't crush my poor fingers. I fled from those pirates at the wharf, Jack, instead of waiting to offer you my most humble thanks. Will you accept them now? They come straight from the heart."

For such a reward as this Jack would have fought a dozen pirates. Baring his head, he murmured bashfully:

"A trifling service, Mistress Dorothy, and 'tis my devout hope that I may always be ready in time of need."

"So?" she exclaimed, with mischief in her eyes. "I believe you would slay a pirate each morning before breakfast, should I ask it."

"Or any other small favors like that," gallantly returned Jack.

"A proper courtier," cried Dorothy. "My father will thank you when he returns from North Carolina. When I ventured to the wharf this morning it was in hopes of sighting his armed sloop."

The dwelling of Mr. Peter Arbuthnot Forbes was at some distance from the tavern which was on the sloping ground that overlooked the harbor, among the spreading live-oaks and magnolias. Borne on the breeze came the sounds of Stede Bonnet's pirates at their revels, pistol shots, wild choruses, drunken yells. Jack was not disturbed although Mistress Dorothy moved closer and laid a hand on his arm. Presently the tumult ceased, abruptly, and now Jack was perplexed. It might mean a sudden recall to the ship. Something was in the wind. The youth and the maid stood listening. Jack was about to scramble to the roof of the house in order to gaze toward the harbor but Dorothy bade him stay with her. Her fair cheek had paled and she shivered with a vague apprehension.

This sudden stillness was uncanny, threatening. Soon, however, a trumpet blew a long, shrill call to arms, and they heard one hoarse, jubilant huzza after another.

"Have Stede Bonnet's pirates mustered to sack the town?" implored Dorothy.

"I can speedily find out," replied her protector.

"Oh, I pray you not to leave me," she tremulously besought him.

"Captain Bonnet will wreak no harm on Charles Town," Jack assured her. "I know him too well for that. You saw what he did to the base varlet who annoyed you at the wharf,—felled him like an ox."

"If only my father were here, to call out the troops and rout this rabble of sea rogues, Jack dear," was her fluttering prayer.

A little after this, the tumult increased and it was drawing nearer. It was a martial clamor of men on the march, with the rattle of drums and a loud fanfare of trumpets. Mr. Peter Arbuthnot Forbes came running out of the house, all flustered and waving his hands, and ordered the two young people indoors. The servants were closing the heavy wooden shutters and sliding the bars across the doors.

Jack slipped out into the lane and hailed a neighbor who dashed past. The news was babbled in fragments and Jack scurried back to blurt to his uncle:

"An Indian raid,—the savages are within a dozen miles of Charles Town, laying waste the plantations,—slaying the laborers. The militia is called to arms but they lack a leader. Colonel Stuart is sorely missed. Captain Bonnet called another boat-load of his pirates ashore, and they march in the van to assail the Indians. May I go with them, Uncle Peter? Must I play the coward and the laggard?"

"Nonsense, John Cockrell. These mad pirates have addled your wits. Shall I let you be scalped by these painted fiends of Yemassees?"

"Then you will volunteer in my stead," shrewdly ventured Jack, with a glance at Dorothy.

"Um-m. Duty and my official cares prevent," quoth the worshipful Secretary of the Colony, frowning and pursing his lips. Dorothy smiled at this and winked at Jack. Uncle Peter was rated a better lawyer than a valiant man of war.

"Let us stand at a window," exclaimed the girl. "Ah, they come! My faith, but this is a brave array. And Captain Bonnet leads them well."

She had never expected to praise a pirate but there was no denying that this lean, straight rover in the scarlet coat and great cocked hat looked the part of a competent and intrepid soldier. He was superbly fit for the task in hand. Catching sight of Jack Cockrell and Dorothy Stuart in the window, he saluted by raising the hilt of his cutlass and his melancholy visage brightened in a smile.

Behind him tramped his men in column of fours, matchlocks across their shoulders, bright weapons swinging against their thighs as they sang all together and kept step to the beat of the drums.

"But ere to Execution Bay,
The wind these bones do blow,
I'll drink an' fight what's left away,
Yo, ho, with the rum below."

Behind these hardy volunteers straggled as many of the militia company as had been able to answer the sudden call, merchants, clerks, artisans, and vagabonds who seemed none too eager to meet the bloodthirsty Yemassees. Their wives and children trailed after them to the edge of the town, amidst tears and loud lamentations. The contrast did not escape the eye of Mr. Peter Arbuthnot Forbes who reluctantly admitted:

"Give the devil his due, say I. These wicked brethren of the coast go swaggering off of their own free will, as though it were to a frolic. I will remember it in their favor when they come to hang."

A long roll of the drums and a lilting flourish by the pirate trumpeter as a farewell to Charles Town and its tavern and its girls, and the company passed from view. The lane was again deserted and silent and Jack offered to escort Dorothy Stuart to her own home. As they loitered across an open field, he cried in a fierce flare of rebellion:

"My good uncle will drive me too far. Let him sail for old England and leave me to find my own career. Upon my soul, I may run away to join a pirate ship."

Dorothy tried to look grave at this dreadful announcement but a dimple showed in her cheek as she replied:

"My dear Jack, you can never be braver but you will be wiser some day. Banish such silly thoughts. You must obey your lawful guardian."

"But did you see the lads in the militia company? Two or three of them I have whipped in fair fight. And Uncle Peter wants to keep me tucked in a cradle."

"Softly, Jack," said she, with pretty solicitude. "Stede Bonnet has bewitched you utterly."

The stubborn youth shook his head. This day of humiliation had been the last straw. He was ripe for desperate adventure. It would have made him happy and contented to be marching against the Indians with Stede Bonnet and his cut-throats, in peril of tomahawks and ambuscades.

Small wonder that poor Jack Cockrell's notions of right and wrong were rather confused, for he lived in an age when might ruled blue water, when every ship was armed and merchant seamen fought to save their skins as well as their cargoes. English, French, Spanish, and Dutch, they plundered each other on the flimsiest pretexts and the pirates harried them all.

Still sulky, Jack betook himself to the rectory next morning for his daily bout with his studies. Parson Throckmorton was puttering in the garden, a shrunken little man who wore black small-clothes, lace at his wrists, and a powdered wig. Opening the silver snuff-box he almost sneezed the wig off before he chirruped:

"Ye mind me of Will Shakespeare's whining schoolboy, Master John,—creeping like snail unwillingly to school. A treat is in store for us to-day, a signal treat! We begin our Virgil. *'Arma virumque cano.'*"

"Arms and a man? I like that much of it," glowered the mutinous scholar, "but my uncle makes me sing a different tune."

"He accepted my advice,—that you be educated in England," said the parson.

"Then I may hold you responsible for this hellish thing?" angrily declaimed Jack. "Were it not for your white hairs——"

He subsided and had the grace to apologize as they entered the library. The tutor was an impatient old gentleman and the pupil was so inattentive that his knuckles were sharply rapped with a ruler. A blunder more glaring and the ruler came down with another whack. This was too much for Jack who jumped up, rubbed his knuckles, and shouted:

"Enough, sir. I would have you know that I all but killed a big, ugly pirate yesterday."

"So rumor informs me," rasped Parson Throckmorton, "but you will give yourself no grand airs with me. Construe this passage properly or I must tan those leather breeches with a limber rod."

This was too much for the insulted Jack who slammed down the book, clapped on his hat, and tramped from the room in high dudgeon. Such scurvy treatment as this was fairly urging him to a life of crime on the rolling ocean. He wandered down to the wharf and wistfully gazed at the lawless brig, *Royal James*, which swam at her anchorage in trim and graceful beauty. A few men moved briskly on deck, painting the bulwarks or polishing brass. Evidently Stede Bonnet had sent off word to be all taut and ready to hoist sail for another cruise.

After a while the truant went homeward and manfully confessed to the quarrel with Parson Throckmorton. Uncle Peter Forbes was amazingly mild. There was no gusty outbreak of temper and, in fact, he had little to say. It was in his mind to patch up a truce with his troublesome nephew pending their departure for England. He even suggested that the studies be dropped and advised Jack to go fishing in his canoe.

Several days later, Captain Bonnet and his pirates came back from their foray against the Indians. They were a foot-sore, weary band, the wounded carried in litters and several men missing. Their gay garments were caked with mud, the finery all tatters, and most of them were marked with cuts and scratches, but they pulled themselves together and swaggered into Charles Town as boldly as ever to the music of trumpet and drum. Stede Bonnet carried an arm in a sling. As he passed the Secretary's house he cheerily called out to Jack:

"Ahoy, my young comrade! 'Twill please you to know that fair Mistress Dorothy Stuart may sleep in peace."

"Did you scatter the savages, sir?" asked Jack, running out to shake his hand.

"God bless ye, boy, we exterminated 'em."

The gratitude of Mr. Peter Arbuthnot Forbes was stronger than his dislike and he came out to thank the captain in behalf of the citizens of Charles Town. To his excited questions the pirate replied:[33]

"There be old buccaneers from Hispaniola in my crew, may it please Your Excellency,—fellows who hunted the Indians in their youth,— their time with the log-wood cutters of Yucatan. They laughed at the tricks of these Yemassees of the Carolinas."

One of the militia company broke in to say to Mr. Forbes:

"Your Honor's own plantation was saved from the torch by this doughty Captain Bonnet. It was there he pulled the flint arrow-head from his arm and was near bleeding to death."

Mr. Peter Forbes could do no less than invite the pirate into the house, for the wounded arm had been rudely bandaged and was in sore need of dressing. Jack fetched a tray of cakes and wine while his uncle bawled at the servants who came running with soft cloths and hot water and healing lotions. Captain Bonnet protested that the hurt was trifling and carelessly explained:

"My own ship's surgeon was spitted on a boarding-pike in our last action at sea and I have not found me another one. You show much skill and tenderness, sir."

"The wound is deep and ragged. Hold still," commanded Mr. Peter Forbes. "You have been a soldier, Captain Bonnet, commended for valor on the fields of Europe and holding the king's commission. Why not seek pardon and serve with the armed forces of this province? My services in the matter are yours to command."

Stede Bonnet frowned and bit his lip. All he said was:

"You meddle with matters that concern you not, my good sir. I am a man able to make my own free choice."

"Captain Bonnet does honor to the trade of piracy," cried the admiring Jack, at which his uncle declared, with a wrathful gesture:

"I must remove this daft lad to England to be rid of you, Stede Bonnet. You have cast a wicked spell over him."

"To England?" said the pirate, with a sympathetic glance at the boy. "I would sooner lie in gaol."

"And reap your deserts," snapped Uncle Peter.

"No doubt of that," frankly agreed the pirate. "And what thinks the lad of this sad penance?"

"I hate it," was Jack's swift answer. "Will you grant our merchant ship safe conduct, Captain Bonnet?"

"What ship, boy? You have only to name her. She will go scathless, as far as in my power."

"The *Plymouth Adventure*," replied Jack. "It would ruin my uncle's temper beyond all mending to be taken by pirates."

"I pledge you my word," swore Stede Bonnet. "Moreover, if trouble befall you by sea or land, Master Cockrell, I pray you send me tidings and you will have a friend in need."

That night those who dwelt near the harbor heard the clank of a windlass as the crew of the *Royal James* hove the cable short, and the melodious, deep-throated refrain of a farewell chantey floated across the quiet water. With the flood of the tide and a landward breeze, the brig stole out across the bar while the topsails were sheeted home. When daylight dawned, she had vanished in the empty reaches of the Atlantic.

The brig sailed without Jack Cockrell. His shrewd uncle saw to that. It was not by accident that a constable of the town watch loitered in the lane by the Secretary's house. And Uncle Peter himself was careful not to let the lad out of his sight until the beguiling Stede Bonnet had left his haunts in Charles Town. Life resumed its routine next day but the boy's whole current of thought had been changed. He was restless, craving some fresh excitement and hoping that more pirates might come roaring to the tavern green.

He found welcome diversion when the *Plymouth Adventure*, merchant trader, arrived from London after a famous passage of thirty-two days to the westward. Her master's orders were to make quick dispatch and return with freight and passengers direct from Charles Town. Jack was given no more leisure to brood over his own misfortunes. There were many errands to be done for Mr. Peter Forbes, besides the chests and boxes to be packed and stoutly corded. As was the custom, they had to supply their own furniture for the cabin in the ship and Jack Cockrell enjoyed the frequent trips aboard.

He found much to interest him in the sedate, bearded Captain Jonathan Wellsby of the *Plymouth Adventure*, in the crew of hearty British tars who feared neither man nor devil, in the battery of nine-pounders, the stands of boarding-pikes, and the triced hammock nettings to protect the vessel against hand-to-hand encounters with pirates. The voyage might be worth while, after all. There were to be a dozen of passengers, several ladies among them. The most distinguished was Mr. Peter Arbuthnot Forbes, Secretary of the Provincial Council, who was accorded the greatest respect and given the largest cabin.

It was an important event when the *Plymouth Adventure* hoisted all her bunting on sailing day and Charles Town flocked to the harbor with wistful envy of the lucky people who were bound home to old England. There were sad faces among those left behind to endure the perils, hardships and loneliness of pioneers. Jack Cockrell's heart beat high when he saw sweet Dorothy Stuart in the throng. He tarried ashore with her until the boatswain's pipe trilled from the *Plymouth Adventure* to summon the passengers on board. Colonel Stuart, blonde and bronzed and stalwart, escorted his winsome daughter and he praised Jack for his deed of courage, telling him:

"There will soon be fewer pirates for you to trounce, I hope, my lad."

"The town will be a stupid place without a visit from the jolly rovers now and then," honestly replied Jack, at which Colonel Stuart laughed and his daughter suggested:

"With my brave knight in distant England, deliver me from any more pirates."

Jack blushed and was both happy and sad when the dear maid took a flower from her bodice and gave it to him as a token of remembrance. He solemnly tucked it away in a pocket, stammered his farewells, and went to join his uncle who waited in the yawl at the wharf. Once on board the *Plymouth Adventure*, they were swept into a bustle and confusion. Captain Jonathan Wellsby was in haste to catch a fair wind and make his offing before nightfall. His sailors ran to and fro, jumping at the word, active and cheery. Stately and slow, the high-pooped merchant trader filled away on the larboard tack and pointed her lofty bowsprit seaward.

The watches were set, ropes coiled down, and the tackles of the cannon overhauled. The skipper paced the after-deck, a long telescope under his arm, while the passengers lined the rail and gazed at the rude settlement that was slowly dropping below the horizon. The sea was tranquil and the breeze steady. The ship was clothed in canvas which bellied to drive her eastward with a frothing wake. Safely she left the outer bar astern and wallowed in the ocean swell.

The afternoon sun was sinking when a sail gleamed like a bit of cloud against the southerly sky. Captain Wellsby held to his course and showed no uneasiness. Soon another sail became visible and then a third, these two smaller than the first. They might be honest merchantmen steering in company, but the skipper consulted with his mates and the spy-glass passed from hand to hand. The passengers were at supper in the cuddy and their talk and laughter came through the open skylights.

Presently the boatswain piped the crew to quarters and the men moved quietly to their battle stations, opening the gun-ports and casting loose the lashings. The boys fetched paper cartridges of powder in buckets from the magazine and the gunners lighted the matches of tow. Cutlasses were buckled on and the pikes were scattered along the bulwarks ready to be snatched up.

It was impossible to escape these three strange vessels by beating back to Charles Town, for the *Plymouth Adventure* made lubberly work of it when thrashing to windward. She was a swift ship, however, before a fair wind, and Captain Wellsby resolved to run for it, hoping to edge away from danger if his suspicions should be confirmed.

Before sunset the largest of the strange sail shifted her course as though to set out in chase and overhaul the deep-laden merchant trader. Captain Wellsby stood near the tiller, his hands clasped behind him, a solid, dependable figure of a British mariner. The passengers were crowding around him in distressful agitation but he calmly assured them a stern chase was a long chase and he expected to slip away under cover of night. So far as he was aware, no pirates, excepting Stede Bonnet, had been recently reported in these waters.

Here Mr. Peter Forbes broke in to say that the *Plymouth Adventure* had naught to fear from Captain Bonnet who had pledged his word to let her sail unmolested. Other passengers scoffed at the absurd notion of trusting a pirate's oath, but the pompous Secretary of the Council could not be cried down. He was a canny critic of human nature and he knew an honorable pirate when he met him.

It was odd, but in a pinch like this the dapper, finicky Councilor Peter Arbuthnot Forbes displayed an unshaken courage as became a gentleman of his position, while young Jack Cockrell had suddenly changed his opinion of the fascinating trade of piracy. He had not the slightest desire to investigate it at any closer range. His knees were inclined to wobble and his stomach felt qualms. His uncle twitted him as a braggart ashore who sang a different tune afloat. The lad's grin was feeble as he retorted that he took his pirates one at a time.

The largest vessel of the pursuit came up at a tremendous pace, reeling beneath an extraordinary spread of canvas, her spray-swept hull disclosing an armament of thirty guns, the decks swarming with men. She was no merchant ship, this was already clear, but there was still the hope that she might be a man-of-war or a privateer. Captain Wellsby looked in vain for her colors. At length he saw a flag whip from the spanker gaff. He laid down the glass with a profound sigh.

The flag was black with a sinister device, a white blotch whose outline suggested a human skull.

Captain Wellsby gazed again and carefully examined the two sloops which were acting in concert with the thirty-gun ship. It was a squadron, and the brave *Plymouth Adventure* was hopelessly outmatched. To fight meant a slaughter with never a chance of survival.

The passengers had made no great clamor until the menacing ship drew close enough for them to descry the dreadful pennant which showed as a sable blot against the evening sky. Two women fainted and others were seized with violent hysteria. Their shrill screams were so distressing that the skipper ordered them to be lugged below and shut in their cabins. Mr. Peter Forbes had plumped himself down upon a coil of hawser, as if utterly disgusted, but he implored the captain to blaze away at the besotted scoundrels as long as two planks held together. The Honorable Secretary of the Council had been too outspoken in his opinions of pirates to expect kindness at their hands.

The sailors also expected no quarter but they sullenly crouched at the gun-carriages, gripping the handspikes and blowing the matches while they waited for the word. The pirate ship was now reaching to windward of the *Plymouth Adventure*, heeling over until her decks were in full view. Upon the poop stood a man of the most singular appearance. He was squat and burly and immensely broad across the shoulders. What made him grotesque was a growth of beard which swept almost to his waist and covered his face like a hairy curtain. In it were tied bright streamers of crimson ribbon. Evidently this fantastic monster was proud of his whiskers and liked to adorn them.

The laced hat with a feather in it, the skirted coat of buff and blue which flapped around his bow-legs, and the rows of gold buttons across his chest were in slovenly imitation of a naval uniform. But there was nothing like naval discipline on those crowded decks where half the crew appeared to be drunk and the rest of them cursing each other.

Captain Jonathan Wellsby smothered a groan and his stern mouth twitched as he said to his chief mate:

"God's mercy on us! 'Tis none other than the bloody Edward Teach,— that calls himself Blackbeard! My information was that he still cruised off the Spanish Main and refitted his ships in the Bay of Honduras."

"The madman of the sea," said the stolid mate. "A bad day for us when he sailed to the north'ard. He kills for the pleasure of it. Now Stede Bonnet loots such stuff as takes his fancy and——"

"He loves to fight a king's ship for the sport of it," broke in the skipper, "but this murderer—— An unlucky voyage for the old *Plymouth Adventure* and all hands, Mate."

One of the women who had been suffered to remain on deck was close enough to overhear the direful news. Her hands to heaven, she wailed:

"Blackbeard! Oh, my soul, we are as good as dead, or worse. Fight and sink him, dear captain. What shall I do? What shall I do? If I had only minded the dream I had the night before we sailed——"

Jack Cockrell sat down beside his uncle, a limp and sorry youth for one who had offered to slay a six-foot pirate before breakfast to please a pretty maid. With a sickly grin he murmured:

"This cockerel crowed too loud, Uncle Peter. Methinks I share your distaste for piracy."

CHAPTER III

HELD AS HOSTAGES TO BLACKBEARD

TO discover the pestilent Blackbeard in Carolina waters was like a thunderbolt from a clear sky. Captain Wellsby had felt confident that he could beat off the ordinary pirate craft which was apt to be smaller than his own stout ship. And most of these unsavory gentry were mere salt-water burglars who had little taste for hard fighting. The master of the *Plymouth Adventure*, so pious and sedate, was a brave man to whom the thought of surrender was intolerable. From what he knew of Blackbeard, it was useless to try to parley for the lives of his passengers. Better it was to answer with double-shotted guns than to beg for mercy.

The British tars, stripped to the waist, turned anxious eyes to the skipper upon the quarter-deck while they quaffed pannikins of rum and water and cracked many a rough jest. They fancied death no more than other men, but seafaring was a perilous trade and they were toughened to its hazards. They were facing hopeless odds but let the master shout the command and they would send the souls of some of these pirates sizzling down to hell before the *Plymouth Adventure* sank, a splintered hulk, in the smoke of her own gunpowder.

Captain Wellsby delayed his decision a moment longer. Something most unusual had attracted his attention. A ball of smoke puffed from a port of Blackbeard's ship, but the round shot splashed beyond the bowsprit of the *Plymouth Adventure* instead of thudding into her oaken side. This was a signal to heave to. It was a courtesy both unexpected and perplexing, because Blackbeard's habit was to let fly with all the guns that could bear as the summons to submit. Presently a dingy bit of cloth fluttered just beneath the black flag. It looked like the remains of a pirate's shirt which had once been white.

"A signal for a truce?" muttered Captain Wellsby. "A ruse, mayhap, but the rogue has no need to resort to trickery."

The two sloops of Blackbeard's squadron, spreading tall, square topsails, came driving down to windward in readiness to fire their bow-chasers and form in line of battle. The passengers of the *Plymouth Adventure,* snatching at the chance of safety, implored the skipper to send his men away from the guns lest a rash shot might be their ruin. They prayed him to respect the precious flag of truce and to ascertain the meaning of it. Mystified and wavering in his purpose, he told the mates to back the main-yard and heave the ship to.

Upon his own deck Blackbeard was stamping to and fro, bellowing at his crew while he flourished a broadsword by way of emphasis. The hapless company of the *Plymouth Adventure* shivered at the very sight of him and yet there was something almost ludicrous in the antics of this atrocious pirate, as though he were play-acting upon the stage of a theatre. He had tucked up the tails of his military coat because the wind whipped them about his bandy legs and made him stumble. The flowing whiskers also proved bothersome, wherefore he looped them back over his ears by means of the bows of crimson ribbon. This seemed to be his personal fashion of clearing for action.

"There be pirates and pirates," critically observed Mr. Peter Forbes as he stared at the unpleasant Blackbeard. "This is a filthy beast, Jack, and he was badly brought up. He has no manners whatever."

"Parson Throckmorton would take him for the devil himself," gloomily answered the lad.

And now they saw Blackbeard raise a speaking-trumpet to his lips and heard the hoarse voice come down the wind with this message:

"The ship ahoy! Steady as ye be, blast your eyes, or I'll lay aboard and butcher all hands."

He turned and yelled commands to the two sloops which now rolled within pistol-shot. In helter-skelter style but with great speed, one boat after another was lowered away and filled with armed pirates. They rowed toward the *Plymouth Adventure* and there wer enough of them to carry her by boarding. In addition to this, she was directly under the guns of Blackbeard's powerful ship. One valorous young gentleman passenger whipped out a rapier and swore to perish with his face to the foe, but Captain Wellsby kicked him into the cabin and fastened the scuttle. This was no time for dramatics.

"It looks that the old ruffian comes on a peaceful errand," said the skipper, by way of comfort. But the hysterical ladies below decks redoubled their screams and one substantial merchant of Charles Town scrambled down to hide himself among them. Mr. Peter Arbuthnot Forbes folded his arms and there was no sign of weakness in his pink countenance. His dignity still sustained him.

As agile as monkeys, the mob of pirates poured over the bulwark, slashing through the hammock nettings, and swept forward in a compact mass, driving Captain Wellsby's seamen before them and penning them in the forecastle. Having cleared the waist of the ship, they loitered there until a few of them discovered the galley and pantry. They swept the shelves and lockers bare of food like a pack of famished wolves. Jack Cockrell looked at them from the poop and perceived that they were a gaunt, ragged lot. The skins of some were yellow like parchment, and fits of trembling overtook them. Something more than dissipation ailed them.

With a body-guard of the sturdiest men, Blackbeard clambered up the poop ladder and, with wicked oaths, told the skipper to stand forth. Clean and trig and carefully dressed, Captain Jonathan Wellsby confronted these savage, unwashed pirates and calmly demanded to know their errand. It was plain to read that Blackbeard thought himself an imposing figure. With a smirk and a grimace he bowed clumsily to a woman on deck who had refused to desert her husband. He growled like a bear at Captain Wellsby and prodded the poor man with his cutlass as he thundered:

"You tried my patience, shipmaster, with your cracking on sail. A little more and I'd ha' slit your throat. Blood an' wounds, would ye dare to vex Blackbeard?"

Captain Wellsby faced him with unshaken composure and returned in a strong voice:

"I beg no favors for myself but these helpless people, women amongst them, came on board with my assurance of safety. They have friends and kinsmen in Charles Town who will ransom them in gold."

Blackbeard's mien was a shade less ferocious as he cried:

"Gold? Can it cool a fever or heal a festering sore? A score of my men are down and the others are tottering ghosts. Medicines I must have. A foul plague on those ports of the Spanish Main which laid my fine lads by the heels."

Jack Cockrell, who had retreated to the taffrail, decided that this unkempt pirate was not so absurd as he appeared. There was the strength of a giant in those hulking shoulders and in the long arms which bulged the coat-sleeves, and the man moved with a quickness which made that clumsy air deceptive. The beard masked his features but the eye was keen and roving, and he had a trick of baring his teeth in a nasty snarl. He uttered no more threats, however, and seemed to be anxiously awaiting the reply of Captain Wellsby, who said:

"The few medicines and simples in my chest will not suffice your need. Your ships are rotten with the Spanish fever."

"A ransom, shipmaster?" exclaimed the pirate. "'Twas in my mind when I flew a white flag for parley. I will hold some of your fine passengers as hostages while the others go in to rake Charles Town for medicines to fetch back to my fleet."

"You will send my ship in?" asked the skipper.

"No! This *Plymouth Adventure* is my good prize and I will overhaul the cargo and sink her at my leisure. My ship will tack in to Charles Town bar. Then let the messengers go in the long-boat to find the store of medicines. Harkee, shipmaster,—two days, no longer, for their return! Failing this, the hostages feed the fishes. Such sport 'ud liven the hearts of my doleful seamen."

It was a shameful bargain, thus to submit to a pirate's whim, but the wretched ship's company hailed it as a glad surprise. They had stood in the shadow of death and this was a respite and a chance of salvation. Captain Wellsby was heart-sick with humiliation but it was not for him to take into his hands the fate of all these others. Sadly he nodded assent. Jack Cockrell nudged his uncle and whispered:

"Why doesn't he sail in with his three ships and take what he likes? The town lies helpless against such a force as this."

"Ssh-h, be silent," was the warning. "He is a wary bird of prey and he fears a trap. He dare not attack the port, since he lacks knowledge of its defenses."

Jack's cheek was rosy again and his knees had ceased to tremble. There was no immediate prospect of walking the plank. To be captured by Blackbeard was a finer adventure than strutting arm-in-arm with Captain Stede Bonnet. It was mournful, indeed, that Captain Wellsby should have to lose his ship but 'tis an ill wind that blows nobody good and the voyage to England, which Jack had loathed from the bottom of his heart, was indefinitely postponed. Such an experience as this was apt to discourage Uncle Peter Forbes from trying it again.

There were sundry chicken-hearted passengers anxious to curry favor with Blackbeard, who gabbled when they should have held their tongues, and in this manner he learned that he had bagged the honorable Secretary of the Provincial Council. The bewhiskered pirate slapped his thighs and roared with glee.

"Damme, but he looks it! Alack that my sorry need of medicines compels me to give quarter! Would I might swing this fat Secretary from a topsail yard! And a rogue of a lawyer to boot! He tempts me—
—"

"I demand the courtesy due a hostage," exclaimed Mr. Peter Forbes.

"Ho, ho, you shall be my lackey,—the chief messenger," laughed Blackbeard, showing his yellow teeth. "Hat in hand, begging medicines for me."

The honorable Secretary was near apoplexy. He could only sputter and cough. He was to be sent as an errand boy to the people of Charles Town, at the brutal behest of this unspeakable knave, but refusal meant death and there were his fellow captives to consider. He thought of his nephew and was about to plead that Jack be sent along with him when Blackbeard demanded:

"What of the boy? He takes my eye. No pursy swine of a lawyer could sire a lad of his brawn and inches."

"I am Master Cockrell," Jack answered for himself, "and I would have you more courteous to my worthy uncle."

It was a speech so bold that the scourge of the Spanish Main tugged at his whiskers with an air of comical perplexity. The headstrong Jack was keen enough to note that he had made an impression and he rashly added:

"'Tis not long since I knocked a pirate on the head for incivility."

Mr. Peter Forbes gazed aghast, with slackened jaw, expecting to see his mad nephew cut down by the sweep of a broadsword, but Blackbeard merely grinned and slapped the lad half-way across the deck with a buffet of his open hand. Dizzily Jack picked himself up and was furiously scolded by his uncle. Their lives hung by a hair and this was no time to play the fool. For once, however, Jack was the wiser of the two. In an amiable humor Blackbeard exclaimed:

"And so this strapping young jackanapes knocks pirates on the head! There be lazy dogs among my men that well deserve it. You shall stay aboard, Master Cockrell, whilst the juicy lubber of a lawyer voyages into Charles Town. He may sweat an' strive the more if I hold you as his security. Zounds, I'll make a gentleman rover of ye, Jack, for I like your mettle."

It was futile for the unhappy uncle to argue the matter. He could only obey the tyrant's pleasure and hope for a speedy return and the release of the terrified passengers. The *Plymouth Adventure* was ordered to haul her course to the westward and jog under easy sail toward the Charles Town bar. Blackbeard was rowed off to his own ship, the *Revenge*, leaving his sailing-master and a prize crew. These amused themselves by dragging the weeping women on deck and robbing them of their jewels and money, but no worse violence was offered. Middle-aged matrons and elderly spinsters, they were neither young nor fair enough to be stolen as pirates' brides.

The *Revenge* and the two sloops hovered within sight of the *Plymouth Adventure* and their sails gleamed phantom-like in the darkness. There was little sleep aboard the captured merchant trader. Some of the pirates amused themselves with hauling chests and boxes out of the cabins and spilling the contents about the deck in riotous disorder. One sprightly outlaw arrayed himself in a silken petticoat and flowered bodice and paraded as a languishing lady with false curls until the others pelted him with broken bottles and tar buckets. By the flare of torches they ransacked the ship for provisions, cordage, canvas, and heaped them ready to be dumped into boats.

Jack Cockrell looked on until he was too drowsy to stay awake and fell asleep on deck, his head pillowed on his arm. Through the night the watches were changed to the harsh summons of the pirate sailing-master or his mate. Once Jack awoke when a seaman staggered into the moonlight with blood running down his face. He was not likely to be caught napping on watch again.

At dawn the *Plymouth Adventure* was astir and the *Revenge* ran close aboard to watch Mr. Peter Arbuthnot Forbes and two prosperous merchants of Charles Town bundled into the long-boat. Blackbeard shouted bloody threats through his trumpet, reminding them that he would allow no more than two days' grace for their errand ashore. Uncle Peter was deeply affected as he embraced his nephew and kissed him on the cheek. Jack's eyes were wet and he faltered, with unsteady voice:

"Forgive me, sir, for all the trouble I have made you. Never did I expect a parting like this."

"A barbarous coast, Jack, and a hard road to old England," smiled the Secretary of the Council. "Have a stout heart. By God's grace I shall soon deliver you from these sea vermin."

The boy watched the long-boat hoist sail with a grizzled, scarred old boatswain from the *Revenge* at the tiller. It drove for the blue fairway of the channel between the frothing shoals of the bar and made brave headway for the harbor. Then the ships stood out to sea to go clear of a lee shore and the captives of the *Plymouth Adventure* endured the harrowing suspense with such courage as they could muster. Should any accident delay the return of the long-boat beyond two days, even head winds or foul weather, or if there was lack of medicines in the town, they were doomed to perish.

Jack Cockrell endured it with less anguish than the other wretched hostages. He had the sublime confidence of youth in its own destiny and he had found a chum in a boyish pirate named Joseph Hawkridge who said he had sailed out of London as an apprentice seaman in a ketch bound to Jamaica. He had been taken out of his ship by

Blackbeard, somewhere off the Azores, and compelled to enlist or walk the plank. At first he was made cook's scullion but because he was well-grown and active, the chief gunner had taken him over as a powder boy.

This Joe Hawkridge was a waif of the London slums, hard and wise beyond his years, who had been starved and abused ever since he could remember. He had fled from cruel taskmasters ashore to endure the slavery of the sea and to be kidnapped into piracy was no worse than other things he had suffered. A gangling lad, with a grin on his homely face, he had certain instincts of manliness, of decent conduct, although he had known only men whose souls were black with sin. Heaven knows where he learned these cleaner aspirations. They were like the reflection of a star in a muddy pool.

It was easy for Jack Cockrell to win his confidence. Few of his shipmates spoke kindly or showed pity for him. And their youth drew them together. Jack's motive was largely curiosity as soon as he discovered that here was one of Blackbeard's crew ready to confide in him. The two lads chatted in sheltered corners of the deck, between watches, or met more freely in the night hours. Jack shuddered at some of the tales that were told him but he harkened breathless and asked for more.

"Yes, this Blackbeard is the very wickedest pirate that ever sailed," said Joe Hawkridge in the most matter-of-fact tones. "You have found him merciful because he fears a mortal sickness will sweep through his ships."

"You have curdled my blood enough for now," admitted Jack. "Tell me this. What do they say of Captain Stede Bonnet? He chances to be a friend of mine."

Joe Hawkridge ceased to grin. He was startled and impressed. Real gentlemen like this young Cockrell always told the truth. Making certain that they could not be overheard, Joe whispered:

"What news of Stede Bonnet? You've seen him? When? Did he cruise to the north'ard? Has he been seen off Charles Town?"

"He came ashore not long ago, and invited me to dinner at the tavern with him," bragged Jack. "And he coaxed me to sign in his ship."

"Yes, you'd catch his eye, Cockrell, but listen! What ship had he, and how many men? God strike me, but I'll not tattle it. I'm true as steel to Stede Bonnet. If you love me, don't breathe it here."

"There is no love lost betwixt him and Blackbeard?" excitedly queried Jack.

"Mortal foes they be, if you ask Stede Bonnet."

Feeling sure he could trust this young Hawkridge, Jack informed him:

"Stede Bonnet flies his pennant in a fine brig, the *Royal James*, with seventy lusty rovers. But what about him, Joe? Why does he hate this foul ogre of a Blackbeard? Did they ever sail together?"

"'Twas in the Bay of Honduras. Captain Bonnet was a green hand at the trade but zealous to win renown at piratin'. And so he made compact with Blackbeard, to sail as partners. There was Stede Bonnet with a fine ship and his own picked crew. By treachery Blackbeard stole the vessel from him. Bonnet and his men were left to shift for 'emselves in a rotten old hulk that was like to founder in a breeze o' wind."

"But they stayed afloat and took them a good ship," proudly exclaimed Jack, with a personal interest in the venture.

"True, by what you say. D'ye see the *Revenge* yonder, Blackbeard's tall cruiser? The very ship he filched from Stede Bonnet by dirty stratagem and broken oaths!"

"Then the powder will burn when next they meet?"

"As long as there's a shot in the locker, Jack. And Blackbeard's men are ripe for mutiny. Let 'em once sight Stede Bonnet's topsails and——"

A gunner's mate broke into this interview with a cat-o'-nine-tails and flogged Joe Hawkridge forward to duty. He ducked and fled with a farewell grin at the nephew of the Secretary of the Council. Now all this was diverting enough to keep Jack from bemoaning his fate, but the other passengers counted the hours one by one and their hearts began to drum against their ribs. They scanned the sea and the harbor bar with aching eyes, for the two days were well-nigh spent and there was never a sign of the long-boat and the messengers with the ransom of medicines which should avert the sentence of death.

Sunrise of the second day brought them no comfort. The sea was gray and the sky leaden, without the slightest stir of wind. The drifting vessels rolled in a swell that heaved as smooth as oil. It was a calm which presaged violent weather. Against her masts the yards of the *Plymouth Adventure* banged with a sound like distant thunder and the idle canvas slatted to the thump of blocks and the thin wail of chafing cordage.

Captain Jonathan Wellsby was permitted the freedom of the poop by Blackbeard's sailing-master who seemed a sober and competent officer. They were seen to confer earnestly, as though the safety of the ship were uppermost in their minds. Soon the pirates of the prize crew were ordered to stow and secure all light sail and pass extra lashings about the boats and batten the hatches. They worked slowly, some of them shaking with fever, nor could kicks and curses and the sting of the whistling cat make them turn to smartly. The sailing-master signaled the *Revenge* to send off more hands but Blackbeard was either drunk or in one of his crack-brained moods. With a laugh he pulled a brace of pistols from his sash and blazed away at the *Plymouth Adventure.*

The two sloops of the pirate squadron had sagged down to leeward during the night and were trying to work back to their stations when the dead calm intervened. Their skippers had sense enough to read the weather signs and had begun to take in canvas. On board of the *Revenge*, however, there was aimless confusion, the mates making some attempt to prepare the ship for a heavy blow while Blackbeard defied the elements. His idea of arousing his men was to try potshots with his pistols as they crept out on the swaying spars.

It was quite apparent that the sailing-master was sorely needed in the *Revenge*, if order was to be brought out of this chaos, but he received no orders to quit the *Plymouth Adventure*. He was a proper seaman, Ned Rackham by name, who had deserted from the Royal Navy, after being flogged and keel-hauled for some trifling offense. Rumor had it that he was able to enforce respect from Blackbeard and would stand none of his infernal nonsense.

"In this autumn season we may catch a storm from the West Indies, Mr. Rackham," said Captain Wellsby. "The sea has a greasy look and this heavy ground swell is a portent."

"The feel of it is in the air, shipmaster. There fell an evil calm like this come two year ago when I was wrecked in a ship-of-the-line within sight of Havana. Four hundred men sank with her."

"If my sailors were not penned in the fo'castle——" suggested the merchant skipper.

"None o' that," was the stern retort. "This ship is a prize to Blackbeard and so she stays, and you will sink or swim with her."

The morning wore on and the two days of grace had passed for those doleful hostages in the *Plymouth Adventure*. They beheld the black flag hoisted to the rigging of the *Revenge* as a signal of tragic import, but the bandy-legged monster with the festooned whiskers was not to disport himself with this wanton butchery. The sky had closed darkly around the becalmed ships, in sodden clouds which were suddenly obscured by mist and rain while the wind sighed in fitful gusts. It steadied into the southward and swiftly increased in force until the sea was whipped into foam and scud.

Staunch and well-found, the *Plymouth Adventure* went reeling off across the spray-swept leagues of water, showing only her reefed topsails and courses. The two pirate sloops vanished beyond the curtain of mist. When last seen, one of them was dismasted and the other was laboring in grave peril. The *Revenge* loomed as a spectral shape while Blackbeard was endeavoring to get her running free in pursuit of the *Plymouth Adventure*. But slovenly, reckless seamanship had caught him unready.

His sails were blowing to ribbons, ropes flying at loose ends, and it was with great difficulty that the vessel could be made to mind her tiller.

Already the sea was rising in crested combers which broke with the noise of thunder and the fury of the wind was insensate. Slowly the struggling *Revenge* dropped astern, yawing wildly, rolling her bulwarks under, splintered spars dangling from the caps. She was a crippled ship which would be lucky to see port again. It was to be inferred that Blackbeard had ceased to cut his mirthful capers on the poop and that he would have given bushels of doubloons to regain his sailing-master and men.

In the *Plymouth Adventure* things were in far better plight, even with the feeble, short-handed prize crew. Prudently snugged down in ample time, with extra hands at the steering tackles, they let her drive. She would perhaps wear clear of the coast and there was hope of survival unless the tempest should fairly wrench her strong timbers asunder.

Lashed to the weather rigging, Captain Jonathan Wellsby wiped the brine from his eyes and waved his arm at the helmsman, now to ease her a little, again to haul up and thus thwart some ravening sea which threatened to stamp his ship under. Sailing-Master Ned Rackham was content to let the skipper con his own vessel in this great emergency.

The mind of Captain Wellsby was very active and he pondered on something else than winning through the storm. He had been helpless while under the guns of the *Revenge*, with the two sloops in easy call. Now the situation was vastly different. He had been delivered out of Blackbeard's clutches. And in the forecastle were thirty British seamen with hearts of oak, raging to be loosed with weapons in their hands.

Peering into the gray smother of sea and sky, Captain Jonathan Wellsby licked his lips hungrily as he said to himself:

"Not now, but if the storm abates and we float through the night, these lousy picaroons shall dance to another tune."

CHAPTER IV

THE CAPTIVE SEAMEN IN THE FORECASTLE

JACK COCKRELL was seasick. This was enough to spoil any adventure. Curled up under a boat, the spray pelted him and the wild motion of the ship sloshed him back and forth. He took no interest even in piracy. Joe Hawkridge, tough as whip-cord and seasoned to all kinds of weather, came clawing his way aft while the water streamed from his thin shirt and ragged breeches. The pirates of the prize crew had sought shelter wherever they could find it. The waist of the ship was flooded with breaking seas. A few of the larboard watch were huddled forward, close to the lofty forecastle where they were stationed as sentries over the imprisoned sailors of the *Plymouth Adventure*.

The commotion of the wind shrieking in the rigging and the horrid crash of the toppling combers were enough to convince a landlubber that the vessel was doomed to founder. But Joe Hawkridge clapped young Jack an affectionate clout on the ear and bawled at him:

> "For his work he's never loth,
> An' a-pleasurin' he'll go,
> Tho' certain sure to be popt off;
> *Yo, ho, with the rum below!*"

Jack managed to fetch a sickly smile of greeting, but had nothing to say. Joe snuggled down beside him and explained:

"I wouldn't dare sing that song if Blackbeard's bullies could hear me. 'Tis known as Stede Bonnet's ditty, for a fight or a frolic."

"By Harry, they can roll it out. My blood tingled when they chorused it through Charles Town," said Jack, with signs of animation and a sparkle in his eye. "Tell me truly, Joe. What about this pirate sailing-master, Ned Rackham? He seems a different sort from your other drunken wretches. He is more like one of Captain Bonnet's choosing."

"Gulled you, has he?" cried Joe. "I was afeard of that. And he's getting on the blind side of your skipper. This Cap'n Jonathan Wellsby is brave enough and a rare seaman, but he ne'er dealt with a smooth rogue like Ned Rackham. He stays sober to plot for his own advantage. He will serve Blackbeard only till he can trip him by the heels. Now listen well, Jack, seasick though ye be. You will have to warn your skipper, Captain Wellsby."

"Warn him of what? My poor head is so addled that I can fathom no plots. How can Ned Rackham do us mischief while this infernal gale blows? He toils with might and main for the safety of the ship."

"Yes, you dunce, and let a lull come," scornfully exclaimed the boyish pirate. "What then? A fine shipthis, and well gunned. She would make a smackin' cruiser for Ned Rackham, eh? He hoists the Jolly Roger on his own account and laughs at Blackbeard."

"Take our ship for his own?" faltered Jack, his wits confused. "I never thought of that. Why, that means getting rid of us, of the passengers and crew."

Joe passed a hand across his throat with a grimace that said more than words.

"He has the ship's company disarmed and helpless, Jack. And pirates a-plenty to work her till he recruits a stronger force. All hands of 'em have a surfeit of Blackbeard's bloody whims an' didoes."

"And Captain Wellsby will be caught off his guard?" said Jack, shivering at the aspect of this new terror.

"Can he do aught to prevent, unless he is bold enough to forestall it?" answered the shrewd young sea waif. "Better die fighting than be slain like squealin' rats."

"Recapture the ship ere Ned Rackham casts the dice," said Jack. "But it means playing the hazard in the midst of this storm. How can it be done? A forlorn venture. It can but fail."

"You are as good as dead if you don't," was Joe's sensible verdict.

Jack Cockrell forgot his wretched qualms of mind and body. The trumpet call of duty invigorated him. He was no longer a useless lump. The color returned to his cheek as he crawled from under the boat and shakily hauled himself to his feet. Joe Hawkridge nodded approval and exhorted:

"A stiff upper lip, my gallant young gentleman. Steady she goes, an' not too hasty. Ned Rackham is as sharp as a whetted sword. Ware ye, boy, lest he pick up the scent. Fetch me word, here, beneath this jolly-boat."

Jack stole away, staggering along the high poop deck until he could cling to the life-line stretched along the roof of the great cabin. There he slumped down and feigned helplessness, banged against the bulwark as a dripping heap of misery or kicked aside by the pirates of the watch as they were relieved at the steering tackles. From half-closed eyes he watched Ned Rackham, a vigilant, dominant figure in a tarred jacket and quilted breeches and long sea-boots. Now and again he cupped his hands and yelled in the ear of Captain Wellsby whose beard was gray with brine.

Jack saw that it was hopeless to get a private word with the skipper on deck. The clamor of the storm was too deafening. The one chance was to intercept him in the cabin when he went below for food and drink. Jack dragged himself to the after hatchway which was shoved open a trifle to admit air, and squeezed himself through. Before he tumbled down the steep staircase he turned to glance at Captain Wellsby. Unseen by Ned Rackham, the boy raised his hand in a furtive, beckoning gesture\

The pirates had taken the main room of the after-house for their own use, driving the passengers and ship's officers into the small cabins or staterooms. The air was foul below, reeking of the bilges, and the main room was incredibly filthy. The pirates ate from dirty dishes, they had scattered food about, and they kicked off their boots to sleep on the floor like pigs in a sty.

Several of them were seated at the long table, bottle and mug in hand, and the gloomy place was poorly lighted by a swinging whale-oil lamp. Jack Cockrell crept unnoticed into a corner and was giddy and almost helpless with nausea. It seemed ages before Captain Wellsby's legs appeared in the hatchway and he came down into the cabin, bringing a shower of spray with him. His kindly face was haggard and sad and he tottered from sheer weariness. Passing through to his own room, a scurvy pirate hurled refuse food at him, with a silly laugh, and others insulted him with the foulest epithets.

He paid them no heed and they returned to their own amusements. Jack Cockrell aroused himself to stumble after the skipper who halted to grasp the lad by the shoulder and shove him headlong into the little room. The door was quickly bolted behind them. A lurch of the vessel flung Jack into the bunk but he managed to sit up, holding his head in his hands, while he feebly implored:

"Did you note me wave my hand, sir, when I came below?"

"Yes, and I followed as soon as I could," answered the master of the *Plymouth Adventure*. "There was the hint of secrecy in your signal, Jack. What's in the wind?"

"I am the only passenger to win the confidence of one of Blackbeard's crew," explained the lad. "This Joe Hawkridge is true to us, I'll swear it. He is a pressed man, hating his masters. He bids me tell you that Ned Rackham will seize the ship for his own as soon as ever the wind goes down."

"Um-m, is he as bold as that?" grunted the skipper, rubbing his nose with an air of rueful surprise. "No honor among thieves, Jack. I thought him loyal to Blackbeard. I have considered attempting something of my own when the weather permits but this news quickens me. This young imp o' Satan that ye call Joe,—he will side with us in a pinch?"

"Aye, sir. And he knows this Ned Rackham well. There has been talk among the pirates of rising against Blackbeard to follow the fortunes of Sailing-Master Rackham. Here is the ship, as Joe says."

"It has a plausible sound," said Captain Wellsby. "My intention was to wait, but I shall have to strike first."

"Can we fight in this storm, sir, even if we manage to release our sailors?" asked Jack, very dismally.

"Not what we can, but what we must do," growled the stubborn British mariner. "The shame of striking my colors rankles like a wound. God helping me, we shall wipe out that stain if we drown in a sinking ship. I talk to you as a man, Master Cockrell, for such you have proven yourself. And who else is there to serve me in this adventure?"

"To set our sailors free, you mean, sir?" eagerly exclaimed Jack. "I took thought of that. There is nobody but me, neither your mates nor the passengers, who can pass among the pirates without suspicion. The knaves have humored me, hearing the tale of the pirate I knocked on the head and my braggart remark to Blackbeard. They have seen me about the decks with Joe Hawkridge as my boon comrade. 'Tis their fancy that I am likely to enlist."

"Well said, Jack," was the skipper's compliment. "Yes, you might make your way for'ard without interference,—but the fo'castle hatches are stoutly guarded. Again, should my brave fellows find exit, they are weaponless, unready. Moreover, they have been crammed in that dark hole, drenched by the sea, cruelly bruised by the tossing of the ship, and weakened for lack of food and air."

"Granted, sir," sighed Jack. "But if some message could be smuggled in to forewarn them of the enterprise,—would that brace 'em to the assault?"

"Will ye try it, Jack?" asked the skipper, with a note of appeal in his hearty voice. "I know not where else to turn. You take your life in your hands but——"

The shipmaster broke off with a grim smile. It was absurd to prate of life or death in such a strait as this. The boy reflected before he said:

"If—if I fail, sir, Joe Hawkridge will try to pass a message in to the men. You can depend on 't."

"A last resort, Jack. You vouch for him but I trust you far sooner. He has kept sorry company."

"When is the best hour, Captain Wellsby?"

"Just before nightfall when the watches will be changing. I dare not delay it longer than that. In darkness, my lads will be unable to find the foe and strike hard and quick. Nor can they rush to lay hold of the only weapons in their reach,—the pikes in the racks beside the masts. Not a pistol or cutlass amongst 'em, and they must fight with these wicked dogs of pirates who think naught of killing men."

"Let your lusty sailors once get clear, sir," stoutly declared Jack Cockrell, "and they will play a merry game with those long pikes. Then I am to slip the message written by your hand on a bit of paper?"

"That's it! I will command them to pound against the scuttle, three raps, for a signal of response, and you must listen for it. Then it is for them to stand ready, on the chance that you can slip the bar of the hatch or the bolts on the door."

"But if they have to come out singly, sir, and the sentries are ready-witted, why, your men may be cut down or pistoled in their tracks."

"I am so aware," said Captain Wellsby, his honest features glum, "but we cannot change the odds."

He found an ink-horn and quill and laboriously wrote a few lines on a leaf torn from the back of a sea-stained log-book. Jack tucked it carefully away and thus they parted company, perhaps to meet no more in life. Through the waning afternoon, Jack stowed himself on deck and held long converse with Joe Hawkridge when they met between the keel-chocks of the jolly-boat. Because he shared not the skipper's feeling of distrust, Jack sought the active aid of his chum of a pirate lad. It was agreed that they should endeavor to reach the forecastle together when the ship's bell tolled the hour of beginning the first night watch.

Joe hoped he might decoy or divert the sentries. If not, he had another scheme or two. A gunner's mate of the prize crew had sent him to overhaul the lashings of the battery of nine-pounders which were ranged along the waist. With several other hands Joe had made all secure, because the guns were apt to get adrift in such weather as this and plunge to and fro across the deck like maddened beasts. Now Joe Hawkridge had lingered, on pretext of making sure that one forward gun could be fired, if needs be, as a distress signal should the ship open her seams or strike upon a shoal.

He had satisfied himself that the tompion, or wooden plug which sealed the muzzle was tight, and that no water had leaked through the wrapping of tarred canvas which protected the touch-hole. Before replacing them, he had made two or three trips to the deck-house amidships in which was the carpenter's room. Each time he tucked inside his shirt as many forged iron spikes, bolts, and what not as he could safely carry.

Unobserved, he shoved this junk down the throat of the nine-pounder and wadded it fast with handfuls of oakum. He worked coolly, without haste, as agile as a monkey when the ship careened and the sea spurted through the cracks of the gun-ports. Well pleased with his task, he said to himself, with that grin which no peril could obliterate:

"God alone knows how I can strike fire to a match and keep it alight, but the sky shows signs of easier weather."

The fury of the storm had, indeed, diminished. It might be a respite before the wind hauled into another quarter and renewed its ferocious violence, but the air was no longer thick with the whirling smother of foam and spray and the straining topmasts had ceased to bend like whips. The ship was gallantly easing herself of the waves which broke aboard and the rearing billows astern were not threatening to stamp her under.

It lacked almost an hour of nightfall when Jack Cockrell crept along the poop and halted to lean against the timbered railing by the mizzen shrouds. All he could think of was that Ned Rackham might seize upon this sudden abatement of the gale to hasten his own wicked conspiracy and so ruin the plan to restore the *Plymouth Adventure* to her own lawful company. This menace had occurred to Captain Jonathan Wellsby who stood tense and rigid at the sailing-master's elbow, watching him from the tail of his eye.

Relief o'erspread the skipper's worn features when he espied Jack Cockrell who stood as if waiting for orders. A nod, a meaning glance, and they understood each other. Striving to appear unconcerned, Jack moved toward the forward part of the ship. He was aquiver with excitement, and his breath was quick and small, but the sense of fear had left him. Captain Wellsby had called him a man and, by God's sweet grace, he would so acquit himself.

The pirates were swarming out of the cabin to taste the clean air and limber their cramped muscles. The ship still wallowed as she ran before the wind and it was breakneck work to clamber about. From the topsail yards fluttered mere ribbons of canvas where the reefed sails had bellied. Ned Rackham shouted for the watch to lay aloft and cut the remnants clear and bend new cloths to keep her from broaching to.

Jack Cockrell's heart leaped for joy. At least a dozen of the most active pirates would have to obey this order. This would remove them from the deck for a precious interval of time. He slouched aimlessly nearer the forecastle, stretching his neck to gaze up at the pirates as they footed the ratlines and squirmed over the clumsy tops. Joe Hawkridge joined him, as if by chance, and they wandered to the lee side of the forecastle. There they were screened from the sight of the sentries.

The wooden shutters of the little windows had been spiked fast on the outside and Jack was at his wits' end to find by what means he might slip the fateful message to the captive seamen. He dared not climb upon the roof and seek for a crack in a hatchway. This would make him too conspicuous.

Cautiously he stole around the massive structure and was all but washed overboard when he gained the windward side where the water broke in hissing cataracts. So great had been its force during the height of the storm, that one of the shutters had been splintered and almost crushed in. Clutching the bit of paper which was tightly rolled and wrapped in a square of oiled linen, Jack pushed it through a ragged crevice in the shutter.

It was gravely doubtful whether the men would discover the message in the gloom of their prison. It might fall to the floor and be trampled unperceived. And yet Jack Cockrell could not make himself believe that deliverance would be thwarted. He said a prayer and waited with his ear against the wall of the forecastle. There he leaned through an agonized eternity as the slow moments passed. It was like the ordeal of a condemned man who hopes that a blessed reprieve may save him, in the last hour, from the black cap and the noose.

Up aloft the pirate seamen were slashing the torn canvas with their dirks and casting loose the gaskets. Presently they began to come down to the deck, one by one. Some whispered word must have passed amongst them, because they drifted aft as by a common impulse although it was not yet the hour to change the watch. Their gunner's mate, a gigantic mulatto with a broken nose, went to the poop when Ned Rackham crooked his finger and these two stood aside, beyond earshot of Captain Wellsby, while they conferred with heads together.

"They will strike first," Jack whispered to himself.

The misty daylight had not darkened. The decks were not yet dusky with the shadows which Jack had hoped might enable him to approach the forecastle door in his brave endeavor to unbar it. The plans were all awry. Tears filled his eyes. And then there came to his ear a muffled knock against the other side of the forecastle planking.

Once, twice, thrice! The signal was unmistakable. A little interval and it was repeated.

Softly the trembling lad tiptoed to the corner of the forecastle house and peered around it to look for the sentries. Two of them had moved a few yards away to join a group which gazed aft as if expecting a summons from Ned Rackham on the poop. The third sentry leaned against the forecastle door, a cutlass at his belt. He was a long, bony man with a face as yellow as parchment from the Spanish fever and it was plain to read that there was no great strength in him.

Faithful Joe Hawkridge sat astride the breech of the nine-pounder at which he had been so busily engaged earlier in the afternoon. He appeared to be an idler who merely looked on but he was watching every motion, and that hard, canny face of his had, for once, forgot to grin. Releasing a three-foot handspike from its lashing beside the gun-carriage, he awaited the next roll of the deck and deftly kicked this handy weapon. It slid toward the forecastle and Jack Cockrell stopped it with his foot.

There was no time for hesitation. Snatching up the iron-shod handspike, Jack rushed straight at the forecastle door. Just then the ship lurched far down and he was shot headlong, like falling off the roof of a house. He had the momentum of a battering-ram. The sentry yelled and drew his cutlass with a swiftness amazing in a sick man. His footing was unsteady or Jack would have spitted himself on the point of the blade. As he went crashing full-tilt into the man the impact was terrific. They went to the deck together and the handspike spun out of Jack's grasp. There was no need to swing it on this luckless pirate for his bald head smote a plank with a thump which must have cracked it like an egg.

Not even pausing to dart after the cutlass which had clattered from the lifeless fingers, Jack spun on his heel and wrenched at the heavy bar across the forecastle door and felt it slide from the fastenings. He tugged it clear and swung himself up to the roof to draw the bolts which secured the hatch. Rusted in their sockets, they resisted him but he spied a pulley-block within reach and used it as a hammer.

All this was a matter of seconds only. The pirates grouped amidships had been waiting for Ned Rackham's word from aft and they were muddled by this sudden shift of action. The other sentries stared in foolish astonishment. The brief delay was enough to let Jack Cockrell free the hatch. While he toiled furiously, several pistols and a musket were snapped at him but the flint sparked on damp powder in the pans and only one ball whistled by his head.

Out of the forecastle hatchway and through the door, the enraged sailors of the *Plymouth Adventure* came rocketing like an explosion. They stumbled over each other, emerging head or feet first, blinking like owls in the daylight but with vision good enough to serve their purpose. Their goal was the nearest stand of boarding-pikes at the foot of the mainmast.

But as they came surging on deck, they were not empty-handed. In the forecastle was a bricked oven for warmth in winter and for cooking kettles of soup. This they had torn to pieces and every man sallied forth with a square, flat brick in each hand and more inside his shirt. Those who were first to gain the deck pelted the nearest pirates with these ugly missiles. The air was full of hurtling bricks and the earliest casualty was a stout buccaneer who stopped one with his stomach.

Driven back in yelling confusion, the pirates found their firearms almost useless, so drenched had the whole ship been by the battering seas, but they were accustomed to fighting it out with the cold steel and they were by no means a panicky mob. The fusillade of bricks held them long enough for the merchant sailors to escape from the forecastle and this was an advantage more precious than Captain Wellsby had hoped for.

What the pirates required was a leader to rally them for attack. Quicker than it takes to tell it, Ned Rackham had raced along the poop and leaped to the waist at peril of breaking his neck. Agile, quick-witted, he bounded into the thick of it, cutlass in hand, while he shouted:

"At 'em, lads! And give the dogs no quarter!"

With hoarse outcry, his gallows-birds mustered compactly while those who had been in the cabin came scampering to join them. Curiously enough, Captain Jonathan Wellsby had been forgotten. He was left alone to handle the ship while the pirate helmsmen stood by the great tiller. To forsake it meant to let the vessel run wild and perhaps turn turtle in the swollen seas. And so the doughty skipper was, for the time, a looker-on.

And now with Ned Rackham in the van, it seemed that the British sailors were in a parlous plight and that their sortie must fail. Craftily the pirates manœuvered to drive them back into the forecastle and there to butcher them like sheep.

CHAPTER V

RELEASING A FEARFUL WEAPON

JACK COCKRELL sprawled flat upon the forecastle roof and knew not what to do. He could lay hands on nothing to serve as a weapon and he bade fair to be trapped like the sailors whose cause he had joined. With a feeling of despair he let his gaze rove to the scrawny figure of Joe Hawkridge who still bestrode the nine-pounder and took no part in the fray. But Joe had no comfort for him, as a gesture conveyed. It had been Joe's wild scheme to obtain the help of Jack and Captain Wellsby, at the least, and so cast loose the gun and slew it around to rake the deck and mow the pirates down. But the men were lacking for this heavy task, and the sailors of the *Plymouth Adventure* were too intent on fighting against fearful odds to pay heed to Joe Hawkridge's appeals. He had even skulked into the galley and was ready with a little iron pot filled with live coals which was hidden under a bit of tarpaulin.

Ned Rackham was a young man and powerful, with a long reach and a skilled blade. He fairly hewed his way into the ruck of the dauntless sailors who had nomore bricks to hurl. Several pirates were disabled, with broken arms or bloody crowns, but the others crowded forward, grunting as they slashed and stabbed, and well aware that Ned Rackham would cut the laggards down should he detect them.

At the moment when there seemed no chance of salvation for the crew of the *Plymouth Adventure*, Joe Hawkridge leaped from the gun and beckoned Jack. The grin was restored to the homely, freckled visage and the salt water gamin danced in jubilant excitement. Down from the forecastle roof tumbled Jack Cockrell and went sliding across the deck, heels over head, to fetch up in the scupper. Joe hauled him by the leg, close to the wooden carriage of the gun, and swiftly told him what was to be done.

Obediently Jack began to loose the knots which secured the rope tackles but it was a slow task. The wet had made the hemp as hard as iron and he lacked a marlinspike. Joe dodged around the gun, saw the difficulty and sawed through one rope after another, all but the last strand or two. Then the lads tailed on to the breeching hawsers, which held the carriage from sliding on its iron rollers, and eased the strain as well as they could.

The ponderous mass was almost free to plunge across the deck. Joe sweated and braced his feet against a ring-bolt while Jack Cockrell found a cleat. Ned Rackham's men were moving forward, cut and thrust, whilethe sailors grappled with them bare-handed and battled grimly like mastiffs.

"The next time she rolls!" panted Joe Hawkridge as the hawser ripped the skin from his palms.

"Aye, make ready to cut," muttered Jack.

The ship heaved herself high and then listed far down to starboard. Joe slashed at the last strands of the tackles and yelled to Jack to let go the hawser. Instead of discharging the nine-pounder, they were employing the piece itself, and the carriage of oak and iron, as a terrible missile. The moment of launching it was shrewdly chosen. The pirates, still in compact formation as led by Ned Rackham, were directly abreast of this forward gun of the main deck battery. The deck inclined at a steep and giddy pitch. With a grinding roar the gun rolled from its station. It gathered impetus and lunged across the ship as an instrument of fell destruction. It was more to be feared than an assault of armed men.

The warning rumble of the iron wheels as they furrowed the planking was heard by the pirates. They turned from their game of butchery and stood frozen in their tracks for a frightened instant. Then they tried to flee in all directions. Their tarry pigtails fairly stood on end. Well they knew what it meant to have a gun break adrift in a heavy sea. Two or three who had been badly hurt were unable to move fast enough. The gun crunched over them and then seemed to pursue a limpng pirate, veering to overtake him as he fled. He was tossed against the bulwark like a bundle of bloody rags.

The gun crashed into the stout timbers of the ship's side and they were splintered like match-wood. It rebounded as the deck sloped sharply in the next wallowing roll, and now this frenzied monster of wood and iron seemed fairly to run amuck. It was inspired with a sinister intelligence, resolved to wreak all the damage possible. The pinnace, the water barrels, the coamings of the cargo hatches, were smashed to fragments as the gun turned this way and that and went plunging in search of victims.

Left to themselves, the seamen of the *Plymouth Adventure* would have risked their lives to cast ropes about the gun and moor it fast. But now they were quick to see that the tide had been turned in their favor. The pirates were demoralized. Some were in the rigging, others atop the bulwarks, and only the readiest and boldest, with Ned Rackham in the lead, had an eye to the task in hand, which was to regain possession of the ship.

And now the boatswain of the *Plymouth Adventure*, a rosy giant of a man from South Devon, shouted to his comrades to follow him. They delayed until the runaway cannon crashed into another gun, and then they broke like sprinters from the mark and sped straight for the mainmast, seeking the rack of boarding-pikes. They ran nimbly, as men used to swaying decks, and compassed the distance in a few strides.

THE BRAWN OF THESE LADS MADE THE PIKE A MATCH FOR A PIRATE'S CUTLASS

Ned Rackham perceived their purpose and tried to intercept but his few staunch followers moved warily, expecting to see that insensate monster of a gun bear down upon them. The swiftest of the merchant sailors laid hands on the pikes and whirled to cover their shipmates, until all hands could be armed. Then the gun came roaring down at them but they ducked behind the mast or stepped watchfully aside. Men condemned to death are not apt to lose their wits in the face of one more peril.

These pikes were ashen shafts with long steel points and the merchant seamen had been trained to use them. And the brawn of these lads made the pike a match for a pirate's cutlass. Ned Rackham bounded forward to swing at the broad, deep-chested boatswain. A wondrous pair of antagonists they were, in the prime of their youth and vigor. The pirate's cutlass bit clean through the pike shaft as the boatswain parried the blow but the apple-cheeked Devonshire man closed in and wrapped his arms around his foe. They went to the deck clutching for each other's throats and the fight trampled over them.

Meanwhile Joe Hawkridge and Jack Cockrell, unwilling to twiddle their thumbs, had rushed aft as fast as their legs could carry them. It was a mutual impulse, to release such of the men passengers as might have a stomach for fighting and also the ship's officers. Into the doorway which led from the waist, the two lads dived and scurried through the main cabin now clear of pirates. Locked doors they smashed with a broadaxe found in the small-arms chest and so entered all the rooms.

The women passengers were almost dead with suffering, what with the turbulence of the storm and the wild riot on deck. The lads pitied them but had no time to console. Several of the men, merchants and planters of some physical hardihood, begged for weapons and Joe Hawkridge bade them help themselves from the spare arms which the pirates had left in the great cabin. In another little room the boys found the mates, steward, surgeon, and gunner of the *Plymouth Adventure* and you may be sure that they came boiling out with a raging thirst for strife.

"Harkee, Jack," said Joe before they climbed to the poop deck, "if the pirates are driven aft, as I expect, they will make a last stand in this cabin house which is like a fort. These 'fenseless women must be hidden safe from harm. Do you coax 'em into the lazarette."

This was a room on the deck below, in the very stern of the ship where were kept the extra sails and coils of rope and various stores. It was the surest shelter against harm in such stress as this. Alas, Jack's persuasions were vain. The frantic women were in no humor to listen, and so the lads bundled them through the hatch as gently as possible and for company gave them such male passengers as lacked strength or courage to join the battle.

While they were thus engaged, two pirates came flying down the ladder from the poop deck into the main cabin. They revolved like windmills in a jumble of arms and legs. Close behind them, in a manner more orderly came Captain Jonathan Wellsby who had tossed the one and tremendously booted the other. They were the helmsmen whom he had replaced with his own officers at the steering tackles, while his first mate had been left in charge of handling the ship.

The skipper was now free to follow his own desires and he fell upon those two stunned pirates in the cabin and trussed them tight with bits of rope. Then he reloaded with dry powder all the pistols he could find and made a walking arsenal of himself. The two lads who now joined him needed no word of command. At his heels they made for the main deck and the shout which arose from those British sailors, so sorely beset, was mightily heartening.

Blazing away with his pistols, the skipper cleared a path for himself, the pirates being taken aback when they were attacked in the rear. And they were leaderless, for Ned Rackham had been dragged aside with the marks of the boatswain's fingers on his throat and a sheath-knife buried in his side. He was alive but nobody paid heed to his groans.

With the skipper in the thick of it, there was no danger of being penned in the forecastle again. The pirates were crowded aft, step by step, before the play of those wicked boarding-pikes. It would be hard to match a sea fight like this, amid the spray and the washing seas, on a deck that tipsily danced and staggered, with a truant gun smashing a good ship to bits and the wounded screaming as they saw this horror thundering at them. Captain Wellsby's men were at pains to drag their helpless comrades to safety but the pirates were too callous and too hard pressed to care for aught save their own worthless skins. They fought like wolves but they lacked the gristle and endurance of the stalwart sailors. Wheezing for breath, they ceased to curse and reeled back in silence while the sailors huzzaed and seemed to wax the lustier.

As was bound to happen, the stubborn retreat broke into a rout. It was every man for himself and the devil take the hindmost. The pirates fled for the after cabin-house, there to take cover behind the timbered walls and use the small port-holes for musketry fire. Thus they could find respite and it would be immensely difficult to dislodge them.

The first mate of the *Plymouth Adventure* and his own two helmsmen saw what was taking place and they were of no mind to be cut off at the stern of the ship. They footed it along the poop and the cabin roof as the pirates were scampering inside and so gained the waist and were with their comrades. The tiller deserted, the vessel careened into the trough of the sea with a portentous creaking of spars and rending of canvas.

The mainmast had been dealt more than one splintering blow by the fugitive gun. This sudden strain, of a ship broached to and hurled almost on her beam ends, was too much for the damaged mast. It broke short off, a few feet above the deck, and the ragged butt ripped the planks asunder as it was dragged overside by the weight of the towering fabric of yards and canvas. One merciful circumstance befell, for the tangle of shrouds and sheets and halliards ensnared the ramping monster of a cannon and overturned it. Caught in this manner, the gun was dragged to the broken bulwark and there it was held with the battered carriage in air.

The mainmast was floating alongside the ship which it belabored with thumps that jarred the hull. It was likely to stave in the skin of the vessel and Captain Wellsby shouted to his men to hack at the trailing cordage and send the mast clear before it did a fatal injury. A dozen men risked drowning at this task while the others guarded the after cabin lest the pirates attempt a sally. These besieged rogues were given an interval in which to muster their force, organize a defense, and break into the magazine for muskets and powder and ball.

Now Captain Wellsby was no dullard and he purposed to make short work of these vile pirates. Otherwise his crippled ship might not survive the wind and weather. He conferred with his gunner who had bethought himself, by force of habit, to fetch from aft his powder-horn and several yards of match, or twisted tow, which were wrapped around his body, beneath the tarred jerkin.

"It grieves me sore to wreck yonder goodly cabin house," said the skipper in his beard, "but, by Judas, we'll blow 'em out of it. Haul and belay your pieces, Master Gunner, and let 'em have a salvo of round shot."

Reckless of the musket balls which began to fly among them, the sailors jumped for their stations at the guns. First they set aright that capsized nine-pounder which had wreaked so much mischief and found that it could be discharged, despite the broken carriage. Joe Hawkridge and Jack Cockrell blithely aided to swing and secure it with emergency tackles and Joe exclaimed, with a chuckle:

"This dose is enough to surprise Blackbeard hisself. 'Tis an ironmonger's shop I rammed down its throat."

The gun was laid on the largest cabin port-hole just as it framed the ugly face of a pirate with a musket while another peered over his shoulder. Joe shook the powder-horn into the touch-hole and the gunner was ready with the match which he had lighted with his own flint and steel. Boom, and the gun recoiled in a veil of smoke. Through the cabin port-hole flew a deadly shower of spikes and bolts while the framework around it was shattered to bits. It was a most unhealthy place for pirates. They forsook it instantly. And the musketry fire slackened elsewhere. It was to be inferred that there was painful consternation in the cabin.

With boisterous mirth, the sailors deftly turned other guns to bear and were careful not to let them get adrift. The muzzles had been well stopped against wetting by the sea and with a little dry powder for the priming, most of them could be served. They could not be reloaded for dearth of ammunition but Captain Wellsby felt confident that one round would suffice.

Methodically the gun-crews aimed and fired one gun after another, watching the chance between the seas that broke aboard. The solid round shot, at short range, ripped through the cabin walls and bulkheads and buried themselves in the frames and timbers of the ship's stern. A good gunner was never so happy as when he saw the white splinters fly in showers and these zealous sailormen forgot they were knocking their own ship to pieces. They were on the target, and this was good enough.

The beleaguered pirates made no more pretense of firing muskets or defying the crew to dig them out. Their fort was an untenable position. At this sport of playing bowls with round shot they were bound to lose. Captain Wellsby sighted the last gun himself. It was a bronze culverin of large bore, taken as a trophy from the stranded wreck of a Spanish galleon. With a tremendous blast this formidable cannon spat out a double-shotted load and the supports of the cabin roof were torn asunder. The tottering beams collapsed. Half the structure fell in.

It was the signal for the sailors of the *Plymouth Adventure* to charge aft and finish the business. They found pirates crawling from under the wreckage. It was like a demolished ant-heap. In the smaller cabins and other rooms far aft, which were more or less intact, some of the rascals showed fight but they were remorselessly prodded out with pikes and those unwounded were hustled forward to be thrown into the forecastle. It was difficult to restrain the seamen from dealing them the death they deserved but Captain Wellsby was no sea-butcher and he hoped to turn them over to the colonial authorities to be hanged with due ceremony.

The badly hurt were laid in the forecastle bunks where the ship's surgeon washed and bandaged them after he had cared for the injured men of his own crew. Ned Rackham was still alive, conscious and defiant, surviving a wound which would have been mortal in most cases. Whether he lived or died was a matter of small concern to Captain Wellsby but he ordered the surgeon to nurse him with special care.

The dead pirates were flung overboard but the bodies of seven brave British seamen were wrapped in sailcloth to be committed to the deep on the morrow, with a round shot at their feet and a prayer to speed their souls. There were men enough to work the ship but she was in a situation indescribably forlorn. It was possible to patch and shore the cabin house and make a refuge, even to find place for the wretched women who were lifted unharmed out of the lazarette. But the stout ship, her mainmast gone by the board, the deck ravaged by that infernal catapult of an errant gun, the hull pounded by the floating wreckage of spars, would achieve a miracle should she see port again.

The combat with the pirates and their overthrow had been waged in the last hour before the gray night closed over a somber sea.

God's mercy had caused the wind to fall and the waves to diminish in size else the ship would have gone to the bottom ere dawn. Much water had washed down into the hold through the broken cargo hatch and the gaps where the runaway gun had torn other fittings away. The carpenter sounded the well and solemnly stared at the wetted rod by the flicker of his horn lantern. The ship was settling. It was his doleful surmise that she leaked where the pounding spars overside had started the butts. It was man the pumps to keep the old hooker afloat and Captain Wellsby ordered his weary men to sway at the brakes, watch and watch.

Joe Hawkridge and Jack Cockrell, more fit for duty than the others, put their backs into it right heartily while the sailors droned to the cadence of the pump a sentimental ditty which ran on for any number of verses and began in this wise:

"As, lately I traveled toward Gravesend,
I heard a fair Damosel a Sea-man commend:
And as in a Tilt-boat we passed along,
In praise of brave Sea-men she sung this new Song,
Come Tradesman or Marchant, whoever he be,
There's none but a Sea-man shall marry with me!"

Thus they labored all the night through, men near dead with fatigue whose hard fate it was to contend now with pirates and again with the hostile ocean. The skipper managed to stay the foremast and to bend steering sails so that the ship was brought into the wind where her motion was easier. The sky cleared before daybreak and the rosy horizon proclaimed a fair sunrise. How far and in what direction the *Plymouth Adventure* had been blown by the storm was largely guesswork. By means of dead reckoning and the compass and cross-staff, Captain Wellsby hoped to work out a position but meanwhile he scanned the sea with a sense of brooding anxiety.

Instead of praying for plenty of sea room, he now hoped with all his heart that the vessel had been set in toward the coast. She was sinking under his feet and would not live through the day. It was useless to toil at the pumps or to strive at mending the shattered upperworks. The men turned to the task of quitting the ship, and of saving the souls on board. It was a pitiful extremity and yet they displayed a dogged, unshaken fidelity. Only one boat had escaped destruction. The pinnace had been staved in by the thunderbolt of a gun and the yawl, stowed upon the cabin roof, was wrecked by round shot. The small jolly-boat would hold the women passengers and the wounded sailors, with the hands required to tend oars and sail.

Nothing remained but to try to knock together one or more rafts. Captain Wellsby discussed it with his officers and it was agreed that the able-bodied pirates should be left to build a raft for themselves, taking their own wounded with them. This was more mercy than they had any right to expect. The strapping young Devonshire boatswain, with his head tied up, was for leaving the blackguards to drown in the forecastle but the shipmaster was too humane a man for that.

It was drawing toward noon when the first mate descried land to the westward, a bit of low coast almost level with the sea. In the light air the sluggish ship moved ever so slowly, with canvas spread on the fore and mizzen masts. Spirits revived and life tasted passing sweet. To drift in the open sea upon wave-washed rafts was an expedient which all mariners shuddered to contemplate. It was with feelings far different that they now assembled spars and planks and lashed and spiked them together on the chance of needing rafts to ferry them ashore from a stranded ship.

Well into the bright afternoon the *Plymouth Adventure* was wafted nearer and nearer the sandy coast. Within a half mile of it a line of breakers frothed and tumbled on a shoal beyond which the water deepened again. The ship could not be steered to avoid this barrier. Her main deck was almost level with the sea which lapped her gently and sobbed through the broken bulwarks. With a slight shock she struck the shoal and rested there just before she was ready to founder.

With disciplined haste, the jolly-boat was launched and filled with its human freightage. The boatswain went in charge and four seamen tugged at the sweeps. There were trees and clumps of bushes among the hillocks of sand and a tiny bight for a landing place. The bulwark was then chopped away so that the largest raft could be shoved into the water by means of tackles, rollers and handspikes. It floated buoyantly and supported as many as fifteen men, who did not mind in the least getting their feet wet. Upon a raised platform in the centre of the raft were fastened barrels of beef and bread and casks of fresh water.

The jolly-boat could hope to make other trips between the ship and the shore but the prudent skipper took no chances with the weather. A sudden gale might pluck the *Plymouth Adventure* from the shoal or tear her to fragments where she lay. Therefore most of the men, including passengers, were embarked on the raft. Captain Wellsby remained aboard with a few of his sailors and our two lads,

Joe and Jack, who had not attempted to thrust themselves upon the crowded raft.

The pirates were making a commotion in the forecastle, yammering to be freed, but the skipper had no intention of loosing them until all his people had safely abandoned ship. The jolly-boat made a landing without mishap and returned to the wreck as the sun went down. More stores were dumped into it, sacks of potatoes and onions which had been overlooked, bedding for the women, powder and ball for the muskets, and other things which it was necessary to keep dry.

Captain Wellsby got rid of the rest of his men on this trip, excepting the gunner and carpenter, and these lingered with him as a kind of body-guard pending the ticklish business of releasing the imprisoned pirates and forsaking them to their own devices. The jolly-boat was laden to the gunwales and Jack Cockrell held back, saying to Joe Hawkridge:

"Why trouble the captain to set us ashore? Let us make a raft of our own. The breeze holds fair to the beach and it will be a lark."

"It suits me well," grinned Joe. "If we wait to go off with the master, and those sinful pirates see me aboard, I'll need wings to escape 'em. They saw me serve the gun that was filled with spikes to the muzzle. Aye, Jack, I will feel happier to be elsewhere when Cap'n Wellsby unbars the fo'castle and holds 'em back with his pistols till he can cast off in the jolly-boat."

"Yes, the sight of you is apt to put them in a vile temper," laughingly agreed Jack, "and 'tis awkward for the master to bother with us. Now about a little raft——"

"Two short spars are enough. There they lie. And the cabin hatch will do for a deck. Spikes for thole-pins, and oars from the pinnace. Unlace the bonnet of the jib for a sail."

"You are a proper sailorman, Joe. A voyage by starlight to an unknown coast. 'Tis highly romantic."

They set to work without delay. Captain Wellsby had occupations of his own and no more than glanced at them in passing. Jack insisted on carrying a water breaker and rations, he being hungry and too busy to pause for supper. They would make a picnic cruise of the adventure. Handily Joe reeved a purchase and they hauled away until their raft slid off the sloping deck to leeward. With a gay hurrah to Captain Wellsby, they paddled around the stern of the ship and through the ruffle of surf that marked the shoal.

In the soft twilight they trimmed the sail and swung at the clumsy oars, while a fire blazing on the beach was a beacon to guide their course. After a time they rested and wiped the sweat from their faces. The progress of the raft was like that of a lazy snail. In the luminous darkness they pulled with all their strength. The wind had died to a calm. The sail hung idle from its yard. They heard, faint and afar, the deep voices of the sailors in the jolly-boat as they returned to take the skipper and his two companions from the ship on which a light burned.

The lads shouted but there came no answering hail from the unseen boat. They were perplexed to understand how their courses could be so far apart. Presently the night breeze drew off the land, bringing with it the scent of green things growing. Joe Hawkridge stared at the fire on the beach and then turned to look at the spark of light on the ship. The raft had drifted considerably to the southward. Anxiously Joe said to his shipmate:

"The flood o' the tide must be setting us down the coast, in some crazy current or other. Mayhap it runs strong through this race betwixt the shoal and the beach with a slant that's bad for us."

"I noted it," glumly agreed Jack. "The jolly-boat passed too far away to please me. And this landward breeze is driving us to sea."

"No sense in breaking our backs at these oars," grumbled Joe. "We go ahead like a crab, with a sternboard. Think ye we can swing the raft to fetch the ship?"

"After Captain Wellsby turns the pirates loose and quits her?" scoffed Jack.

"I am a plaguey fool," cheerfully admitted Joe Hawkridge. "'Twould be out of the frying-pan into the fire, with a vengeance."

"And no way to signal our friends," sadly exclaimed Jack. "We forgot flint and steel. It looks much like another voyage."

"Straight for the open sea, my bully boy," agreed Joe. "And I'd as soon chance it on a hen-coop."

CHAPTER VI

THE VOYAGE OF THE LITTLE RAFT

THESE sturdy youngsters were not easily frightened, and Jack
Cockrell, the landsman, was confident that wind and tide would
change to send the little raft shoreward. So tranquil was the sea that
they rode secure and dry upon the cabin hatch which was buoyed by
the two short spars. Joe Hawkridge was silent with foreboding of a fate
more bitter than the perils which they had escaped. He had seen a lone
survivor of a crew of pirates picked off a raft in the Caribbean, a grisly
phantom raving mad who had gnawed the flesh of his dead comrades.

They drifted quietly before the land breeze, beneath a sky all jeweled
with bright stars. The fire on the beach dimmed to a red spark and then
vanished from their wistful ken. They could no longer see the light on
the wreck of the *Plymouth Adventure*. Now and then the boys struggled
with the heavy oars and rowed until exhausted but they knew they
could be making no headway against the current which had gripped the
derelict raft. They ate sparingly of flinty biscuit and leathery beef
pickled in brine and stinted themselves to a few swallows of water from
the wooden breaker or tiny cask.

"Hunger and thirst are strange to ye, Jack," said young Hawkridge as
they lay stretched side by side. "Hanged if I ever did get enough to eat
till I boarded the *Plymouth Adventure*. Skin and bone I am. I'll not call
this a bad cruise unless we have to chew our boot-tops. A pesky diet is
leather. I've tried it."

"Truly, Joe?" cried Jack in lugubrious accents. "We may have more
heart when morning comes. A piping easterly breeze, such as is wont to

come up with the sun in Charles Town, and we can steer for the coast all taut and cheery."

"I dread the sun, Jack. For men adrift the blaze of it fries them like fish on a grid. A pint of water a day, no more, is the allowance. 'Twill torture you, but castaways can live on it. They have done it for weeks on end. Here's two musket balls in my pocket. I can whittle a balance from a bit of pine and we must weigh the bread and meat."

"Two musket balls' weight of food for a meal?" protested Jack.

"Not a morsel more," was the grim answer. "Granted we be not washed off this silly raft and drowned when a fresh breeze kicks up the sea, we may hold body and soul together through five or six days."

"But some vessel will sight us, Joe, even if the plight is as dark as your melancholy fancies paint it. And I thought you a light-hearted mariner in danger."

"The sea is a cruel master and she hath taught me prudence," was the reply. "A vessel sight us? I fear an empty sea so soon after the storm. And honest ships will be loth to venture out from port if the word sped that Blackbeard was cruising off Charles Town bar."

Jack Cockrell forsook the attempt to wring comfort out of his hardy companion who refused to delude himself with vain imaginings. However, it is the blessed gift of youth to keep the torch of hope unquenched and presently they diverted themselves with chatting of their earlier adventures. Jack was minded of his pompous, stout-hearted uncle, Mr. Peter Arbuthnot Forbes, and wondered how he had fared, whether he had set out to return to Blackbeard's ship with the store of medicines from Charles Town when the great storm swooped down.

Forgotten were Jack's hot grievances against the worthy Secretary of the Council who had sought to take a father's place. Piracy had lost its charm for young Master Cockrell and meekly would he have obeyed the mandate to go to school in merry England among sober, Christian folk.

"Tremendous odd, I call it," exclaimed Joe Hawkridge. "Here I was a pirate and hating the dirty business. And my dreams were all of learnin' to be a gentleman ashore, to know how to read books and such. Blow me, Jack, we should ha' swapped berths."

"If my good uncle is alive I mean to commend you to his kindness," exclaimed Jack. "We must cleave together, and you shall have a skinful of books and school and manners."

This pleased the young sea rover beyond measure and he diverted himself with pictures of a cleaner, kindlier world than he had ever known. In the small hours of the night, the twain drowsed upon their frail platform which floated as a speck on the shrouded ocean. The waves splashed over the spars as the breeze grew livelier and the piteous voyagers were sopping wet but the water was not chill and they slept through this discomfort.

Jack Cockrell dreamed of walking in a green lane of Charles Town with lovely Dorothy Stuart. A wave slapped his face and he awoke with a sputtering cry of bewilderment. The eastern sky was rosy and the sea shimmered in the eternal beauty of a new day. Joe Hawkridge sat huddled against the mast, chin and knees together, his sharp eyes scanning the horizon. With a grin he exclaimed:

"The watch ahoy! Rouse out, shipmate, and show a leg! Turn to cheerly! Holystone decks and wash down, ye lazy lubber."

Jack groaned and scowled as he rolled over to ease his aching bones. He was in no mood for jesting. There was no land in sight nor the gleam of a sail, naught but the empty waste of the Atlantic, and the wind still held westerly.

"Let's have the beggarly morsel you miscall breakfast, Joe, and a swig from the breaker. Are we bound across the main?"

"Straight for London River, and the school you prate about, my bucko," replied the scamp of a pirate. "Haul away on your belt and set the buckle tighter. 'Twill ease the cursed hunger pain that gnaws like a rat."

They munched the pittance of salty food which made the thirst the harder to endure, and then watched the sun climb hot and dazzling. It was futile to hoist the sail and so they pulled the canvas over them as the heat became more intense. By noon, Jack was begging for water to lave his tongue but Joe Hawkridge laughed him to scorn and swore to hit him with an oar unless he changed his tune. Never in his life had Jack known the lack of food or drink and he therefore suffered cruelly.

Worse than this privation was the increasing roughness of the sea. It was a blithesome wind, rollicking across a sparkling carpet of blue, with the little white clouds in flocks above, like lambs at play. But the raft was more and more tossed about and the waves gushed over it like foam on a reef. Through the day the castaways might cling to it but they dreaded another night in which their weary bodies could not possibly ward off sleep. Even though they tied themselves fast, what if the raft should be capsized by the heave of the mounting swell? It was the merest makeshift, scrambled together in haste as a ferry from the wreck of the *Plymouth Adventure.*

No longer did Jack Cockrell bemoan his situation. Taking pattern from his comrade in misery, he set his teeth to await the end as became a true man of gentle blood. After all, drowning was easier than the slow torments of hunger and thirst.

Every little while one of them crawled from under the canvas to look for a ship. It was the vigilant Joe Hawkridge who, at length, discovered what was very like a fleck of cloud on the ocean's rim, to the southward. Afraid that his vision tricked him, he displayed no emotion but held himself as steady as any stoic. Jack was wildly excited, blubbering and waving his arms about. His hard-won composure was broken to bits. But even though it were a ship, Joe well knew it might pass afar off and so miss sighting this bit of raft which drifted almost submerged.

Slowly the semblance of a wandering fragment of cloud climbed the curve of the watery globe until Joe Hawkridge perceived, with a mariner's eye, that it was, indeed, a vessel steering in their direction.

"Two masts!" said he, "and to'gallant-sails set to profit by this brave breeze. A brig, Jack! Had she been a ship, my heart 'ud ha' been in my throat. Blackbeard's *Revenge* might be working up the coast, did she live through the storm."

"A brig?" joyfully cried Jack. "Ah, ha, I see her[two masts plainly, with mine own eyes. And they soar too tall for a merchant trader. Her sails, too,—she spreads them like great wings. Who else will it be than Captain Stede Bonnet in the *Royal James?*"

"A shift of luck is due us, by the bones of Saint Iago," shouted Joe, in a thrill of glad anticipation. "Watch her closely. You saw the brig in Charles Town harbor. Bless God, this may well be Cap'n Stede Bonnet yonder, an' perchance he cruises in search of Blackbeard to square accounts with that vile traitor that so misused him."

"A sworn friend of mine is Stede Bonnet," proudly declared Jack Cockrell, "and pledged to bear a hand when I am in distress. He will land us safe in Charles Town, Joe,—unless,—unless we choose to go a-piratin' with him in the *Royal James*——"

Jack's voice trailed off in tones of indecision so comical that his comrade cried:

"Not cured yet, you big numbskull? 'Cause this fine Cap'n Bonnet is a gentleman pirate? His neck will stretch with the rest of 'em when the law overtakes him. Thirteen burly lads I saw swinging in a row at Wapping on the Thames."

"I'll not argue it," sheepishly mumbled Jack. "However, we'll find a safe deliverance aboard this *Royal James*."

They clung to the swaying raft while the water washed over their knees and watched the two masts disclose themselves until they fancied they could not be mistaken. No other brig as powerful as this had been reported cruising in the waters of Virginia and the Carolinas. By a stroke of fortune almost incredible they had been saved at the very brink of death. The brig was steering straight toward them, hauled to take the wind abeam, and she would be up before sunset.

Shading his eyes with his hand, Joe Hawkridge suddenly uttered a curse so fierce and wicked that it was enough to freeze the blood. He clutched Jack's shoulder for support as though shorn of all his strength and hoarsely gasped:

"Not two masts but three! See it? She lifts high enough to show the stump of the foremast with head-sails jury rigged. 'Twas the storm made a brig of her!"

"Then she may be Blackbeard's ship?" faltered Jack, in a whisper.

"Remember when the gale first broke and we parted company?" was the reply. "The *Revenge* lost her fore-topmast ere the swine could find their wits."

"Aye, Joe, but this may be some other vessel."

"She looks most damnably familiar," was the reluctant admission. "A great press of sail,—it fooled me into thinking her Stede Bonnet's brig."

Gloomily they waited until the black line of the hull was visible whenever the raft lifted on the back of a wave. This was enough for Joe. He recognized the graceful shear of the flush deck which had been extended fore and aft to make room for a heavier main battery. Even at a distance, a sailor's eye could read other signs that marked this ship as the *Revenge*.

"The devil looks after his own," angrily exclaimed Joe. "I'd ha' wagered my last ducat that she was whirled away to founder. Blackbeard boasts of his compact with Satan. I believe it's true."

"Shall we pull down our mast and pray that he passes the raft as a piece of wreckage?" implored Jack.

Mustering his wits to meet this new crisis, Joe Hawkridge cried impatiently:

"No, no, boy! This way death is sure, and most discomfortin'. If it suits Blackbeard's whim to pick us up, there is a chance,—a chance, I say, but make one slip and he will run us through with his own hand."

"We must arrange our tale of the wreck, Joe, to match without flaw. Quick! What have we to say?"

"A task for a scholar, this," grinned the sea urchin. "If it's not well learned, we'll taste worse'n a flogging. Where be his prize crew of pirates, asketh Blackbeard. Answer me that, Jack."

"The *Plymouth Adventure* was driven upon a shoal and lost," glibly affirmed the other lad who had rallied to play at this hazardous game. "Her boats were stove up. We left the pirates building a raft for themselves and trusted ourselves to this poor contrivance, hoping to gain the coast."

"Good, as far as it goes," observed the critical Joe.

"And it veers close to the truth. About the ship's company? What say you?"

"There I hang in the wind," confessed Jack. "Blackbeard would have flung 'em overboard, I trow. Have a shot at it yourself."

"Well, leave me to answer that when the time comes. That we may agree, suppose we say Ned Rackham needed the sailors to work the ship and so spared 'em. Hanged if we can make it all true as Gospel."

"But if Blackbeard searches for the wreck, or if some of those pirates rejoin him, Joe——"

"But me no more buts," snapped the sea rover. "We be jammed in a clove-hitch, as the seaman's lingo hath it. Take trouble as it comes and, ware ye, don't weaken."

They stared at the oncoming ship, dreading to be rescued and even more fearful of being passed by. Disfigured though she was by a shattered foremast, the *Revenge* made a gallant picture as she leaned to show the copper sheathing which flashed like gold. Her bow flung the crested seas aside and Joe Hawkridge muttered admiringly:

"A swift vessel! She carries a bone in her teeth. A telescope can sight us soon. Steady the raft, Jack, whilst I wriggle up this mast of ours and wave my shirt."

"A hard choice," sighed Jack. "Now we well know what it means to be betwixt the devil and the deep sea."

They saw the *Revenge* shift her course a couple of points as the sheets were eased off. A little way to windward of the raft, she hove to while a small boat was hoisted out. Curiosity prompted Blackbeard to find out who these castaways were and from what ship they had drifted. It occurred to Joe Hawkridge that he might be in quest of tidings of the two sloops of his squadron which no longer kept him company. Jack Cockrell's teeth chattered but not with cold as the boat bobbed away from the side of the *Revenge*. Presently Joe recognized the pirate at the steering oar as a petty officer who had often befriended him.

This fellow's swarthy, pockmarked face crinkled in a smile as he flourished his broad hat and yelled:

"Stab my gizzard, but here's the London 'prentice-boy a-cruisin' on his own adventure."

"Right-o, Jesse Strawn," Joe called back. "My bark is short-handed. I need lively recruits. Will ye enlist?"

The boat's crew laughed at this as they reached out to lay hold of the raft while the two lads leaped aboard. Joe Hawkridge carried it off with rough bravado as though glad to be among his pals again. They eyed Jack Cockrell with quizzical interest and he did his best to be at ease, permitting Joe to vouch for him as a young gentleman with a taste for piracy who had won Blackbeard's favor in the *Plymouth Adventure*. They were plied with eager questions regarding the fate of the merchant ship and Ned Rackham's prize crew. It was a chance to rehearse the tale as they had concocted it, and it seemed to hang together well enough to satisfy these simple rogues.

In his turn, Joe Hawkridge demanded to know the gossip of the *Revenge*. The storm had sobered Blackbeard, it seemed, and he had displayed the skill of a masterly seaman in bringing them safely through. In toiling for their own lives, the men had forgotten their brawls and plots and guzzling. And the great wind had blown the ship clear of Spanish fever. There were no new cases and the invalids were gaining strength. Fresh food and sweet water were needed and the opinion was that Blackbeard now steered for an old rendezvous of his on the North Carolina coast where his sloops would meet him if they were still afloat.

Jack Cockrell found his courage returning as he clambered up the side of the *Revenge* and followed Joe aft to the quarter-deck. Unless they bungled it, there was a chance that they might escape when the pirates made their landing on the coast to refresh themselves and refit the ship. The mate on watch greeted them good-humoredly enough and bade them enter the cabin where the captain awaited them. Jack was all a-flutter again but he managed to imitate Joe's careless swagger.

Blackbeard lounged at his ease in a huge chair of carven ebony which might have been filched from some stately East Indiaman or a ship of the Grand Mogul himself. He had flung off his coat and the sleeves of a shirt of damask silk were rolled to the elbow. Instead of the great, mildewed sea-boots he wore slippers of crimson leather embroidered with threads of gold. Gorgeous cushions, pieces of plate, costly apparel strewed the cabin in barbaric confusion.

What the two lads gazed at, however, was this bizarre figure of a despot who held the power of life and death. It was one of his quieter interludes when he laid aside the ferocious and bombastic play-acting which made it hard to discover whether he was very cunning or half-mad. The immense beard flowed down his chest instead of being tricked out in gaudy ribbons. He was idly running a comb through it when his small, rum-reddened eyes took in the two lads in dripping clothes who were shoved toward him by the sentry guarding the hatch.

Blackbeard let a hairy hand stray to clutch one of the pistols kept on the table beside him. Jack Cockrell gulped and stole a frightened glance at Joe Hawkridge who winked and nudged him. There was some small comfort in this. Spellbound, they stared at the pistol and then at the pirate's massive forearm on which a skull and cross-bones was pricked in India ink. At this moment Jack earnestly wished himself back on the raft. The barrel of the pistol looked as big as a blunderbuss.

With a yawn, Blackbeard reached for a silver bowl of Brazil nuts, cracked one of them with the pistol-butt and roared for the black cabin boy who came running with a flask of Canary wine and a goblet. Jack

Cockrell's sigh of relief sounded like a porpoise coming up for air. He was not to be shot at once. Suddenly Blackbeard exclaimed, in that husky, growling voice of his:

"I saw you rascals through the glass before I came below. What of the ship I left ye in? Briefly now, and no lies."

Together the lads pieced out the narrative as they had hastily prepared it. The vital thing was to watch lest they tell a word too much. Jack stumbled once or twice but his comrade covered it adroitly, and they did not betray themselves. The sweat trickled into their eyes but the heat of the cabin was excuse for this. Blackbeard studied them intently, munching Brazil nuts and noisily sipping his wine.

"The *Plymouth Adventure* stranded yester-eve?" said he. "Know ye the lay of the coast where the wreck lies? What of the shipmaster and Ned Rackham? Were they able to fix the shoal by reckoning?"

"No, sir," readily answered Joe Hawkridge. "'Twas strange land to all hands."

From a chest Blackbeard hauled out a dog-eared chart of parchment and unrolled it upon the table. The boys foresaw his intention and feared the worst. Presently they heard him mumble to himself:

"A small wind setting from the west'ard,—twenty-four hours of drift for the lads' raft,—a dozen leagues, I call it."

He looked up from the chart to ask:

"The wreck was lodged fast in smooth water and holding together?"

"Aye, but in peril of working off and sinking like an iron pot," answered Joe. "For this reason the people were in haste to quit her."

"Her own crew made for the beach, I have no doubt," shrewdly pursued Blackbeard, "but my men 'ud stay by the wreck and watch the weather ere they shoved off. Trust the food and drink and plunder to hold 'em."

He lumbered to the hatch and called up to the mate on watch. While they conferred, Joe Hawkridge whispered to his perturbed companion:

"He will hunt for the wreck, Jack. But unless the wind changes, he can't beat in to the coast with his fore-topmast gone."

"A merciful delay," muttered Jack. "I worry not so much for Captain Wellsby and his people. They will hide themselves well inland when they make out the *Revenge*, but what of you and me?"

"'Tis a vexing life we lead. I will say that much, Master Cockrell."

CHAPTER VII

THE MIST OF THE CHEROKEE SWAMP

THE dark cloud of anxiety was lightened a trifle by the fact that Blackbeard displayed no ill temper toward the two young castaways. Having obtained such information as they chose to offer, he roughly told them to go forward and join the crew. Whether or no, Jack was impressed as a pirate and it may have amused Blackbeard to recruit by force the nephew of the honorable Secretary of the Provincial Council. For his part, Jack was grateful to be regarded no longer as a hostage under sentence of death. With Joe as an escort who knew the ropes, he went on deck and was promptly kicked off the poop by the mate.

They first found food and quenched their raging thirst with water which had a loathsome smell. Joe reported to the chief gunner and begged the chance to sleep for a dozen hours on end. This was granted amiably enough and the pirates clustered about to ask all manner of curious questions, but the weary lads dragged themselves into the bows of the ship and curled up in a stupor. There they lay as if drugged, all through thenight, even when the seamen trampled over them to haul the head-sails and tack ship.

When, at last, they blinked at the morning sky, it dismayed them to find the breeze blowing strong out of the southeast and the *Revenge* standing in to the coast under easy sail. They looked aft and saw Blackbeard at the rail with a long glass at his eye. The whole crew was eager with expectation and the routine work went undone. The ship had been put about several hours earlier, Joe learned, and was due soon to sight the shore unless the reckoning was all at fault.

So cleverly had Blackbeard calculated the drift of the boys' raft that a little later in the morning a lookout in the maintop called down:

"Land, ho! Two points off the starboard bow she bears."

"The maintop, ahoy!" shouted Blackbeard. "Can ye see a vessel's spars?"

"'Tis too hazy inshore. But unless my eyes play me tricks, a smudge of smoke arises."

Jack Cockrell nervously confided to Joe:

"That would be Captain Wellsby's campfire on the beach."

"Trust him to douse it," was the easy assurance. "I feel better. Blow me, but I expect to live another day."

"Answer me why," begged Jack. "I am like a palsied old man."

"Well, you know this bit o' coast, how low it setsabove the sea. Despite the haze, a man aloft could see a ship's masts and yards before he had a glimpse of land."

"Then the wreck of the *Plymouth Adventure* has slid off the shoal and gone down, Joe?"

"Yes, when the wind veered and stirred a surf on the shoal. She pounded over with the flood-tide and dropped into fifteen fathom."

"Then we are saved, for now?" joyfully exclaimed Jack.

"Unless we're unlucky enough to find some o' those plaguey pirates afloat on a raft or makin' signals from the beach."

The *Revenge* sailed shoreward until those on board could discern the marching lines of breakers which tumbled across the shoal. The smudge of smoke had vanished from the beach. The lookout man concluded that the haze had deceived him. Blackbeard steered as close as he dared go, with a sailor heaving the lead, but there was no sign of life among the sand-dunes and the stunted trees. And the *Plymouth Adventure* had disappeared leaving no trace excepting scattered bits of floating wreckage.

The pirate ship headed to follow the coast to the northward, on the chance that Ned Rackham's prize crew might have made a landing elsewhere. To Jack Cockrell the gift of life had been miraculously vouchsafed him and he felt secure for the moment. Joe'stheory seemed plausible, that the pirates had abandoned the *Plymouth Adventure* in time to avert drowning with her, and were driven away from the bight and the beach by Captain Wellsby's well-armed sailors.

"Do they know Blackbeard's rendezvous in the North Carolina waters, Joe?" was the natural query. "Are they likely to make their way thither, knowing that honest men will slay them at sight?"

"The swamps and the murderous Indians will take full toll of 'em, Jack. I believe we have seen the last of those rogues, but I'd rest better could I know for certain."

"Meanwhile this mad Blackbeard may be taken in one of his savage frenzies and shoot me for sport," said young Master Cockrell, for whom existence had come to be one hazard after another.

"He seems strangely tame, much like a human soul," observed Joe. "I ne'er beheld him like this. He plots some huge mischief, methinks."

And now the ship's officers drove the men to their work but they were less abusive than usual. They seemed to reflect Blackbeard's milder humor and it was manifest that they wished to avoid the crew's resentment. Joe Hawkridge was puzzled and began to ferret it out among his friends who were trustworthy. They had their own suspicions and the general opinion was that Blackbeard was in great dread of encountering Captain Stede Bonnet in the *Royal James*. It seemedthat the *Revenge* had spoken a disabled merchant ship just after the storm and her skipper reported that he had been overhauled by Stede Bonnet a few days earlier and the best of his cargo stolen. Blackbeard had been seized with violent rage but had suffered the ship to proceed on her way because of his own short-handed condition.

With a prize crew lost in the *Plymouth Adventure*, including Sailing-Master Ned Rackham, and the two sloops of the squadron missing with all hands, the terrible Blackbeard was in poor shape to meet this Captain Bonnet who hated him beyond measure. As if this were not gloomy enough, there were men in the *Revenge* eager to sail under Bonnet's flag and to mutiny if ever they sighted the *Royal James*. It behooved Blackbeard to press on to that lonely inlet on the North Carolina coast and avoid the open sea until he could prepare to fight this dangerous foeman.

It surprised Jack Cockrell to see how quiet a pirate ship could be. The ruffians were bone-weary, for one thing, after the struggle to bring the vessel through the storm. And the scourge of tropic fever had left its marks. Moreover, the rum was running short because some of the casks had been staved in the heavy weather and Blackbeard was doling it out as grog with an ample dilution of water. There was no more dicing and brawling and tipsy choruses. Sobered against their will, some of these bloody-minded sinners talked repentance or shed tears over wives and children deserted in distant ports.

The wind blew fair until the *Revenge* approached the landmarks familiar to Blackbeard and found a channel which led to the wide mouth of Cherokee Inlet. It was a quiet roadstead sheltered from seaward by several small islands. The unpeopled swamp and forest fringed the shores but a green meadow and a margin of white sand offered a favorable place for landing. As the *Revenge* slowly rounded the last wooded point, the tall mast of a sloop became visible. The pirates cheered and discharged their muskets in salute as they recognized one of the consorts which had been blown away in the storm.

Blackbeard strutted on his quarter-deck, no longer biting his nails in fretful anxiety. He had donned the military coat with the glittering buttons and epaulets and the huge cocked hat with the feather in it. He noted that the sloop, which was called the *Triumph*, fairly buzzed with men, many more than her usual complement. No sooner had the ship let her anchor splash than a boat was sent over to her with the captain of the sloop who made haste to pay his compliments and explain his voyage. He was a portly, sallow man with a blustering manner and looked more like a bailiff or a tapster than a brine-pickled gentleman of fortune.

Blackbeard hailed him cordially and invited him into the cabin. The boat waited alongside the *Revenge* and the men scrambled aboard to swap yarns with the ship's crew. Jack Cockrell hovered near the group as they squatted on their heels around a tub of grog and learned that the *Triumph* had rescued the crew of the other sloop just before it had foundered. There were a hundred men of them, in all, crowded together like dried herring, and part were sleeping ashore in huts of boughs and canvas. No wonder Blackbeard was in blither spirits. Here was a company to pick and choose from and so fill the depleted berth-deck of the *Revenge*.

Finding the poop deserted, Joe Hawkridge ventured far enough to peer in at a cabin window. Blackbeard was at table, together with his first mate, the chief gunner, the acting sailing-master, and the captain of the sloop. They were exceeding noisy, singing most discordantly and laughing at indecent jests. Suddenly Blackbeard whipped two pistols from his sash and fired them under the table, quite at random.

The first mate leaped up with a horrible yell and clapped a hand to the calf of his leg. Then he bolted out of the cabin, which was blue with smoke, and limped in search of the surgeon. Joe Hawkridge dodged aside but he heard the jovial Blackbeard shout, with a whoop of laughter:

"Discipline, damme! If I don't kill one of you now and then, you'll forget who I am."

Inasmuch as none of the other guests dared squeak after this episode, it was to be inferred that they were properly impressed.

THE FIRST MATE LEAPED UP WITH A HORRIBLE YELL

In a little while the mate returned with his leg neatly bandaged, announced that it was a mere flesh wound, and sat down as though nothing out of the ordinary had occurred to mar the festive occasion. Through the rest of the day, boats were passing between the ship and the sloop in a convivial reunion. Supper was to be cooked on the beach in great iron kettles and a frolic would follow the feast. The sloop had rum enough to sluice all the parched gullets aboard the *Revenge*.

Jack Cockrell had no desire to join this stupid revel but he was eager to get ashore to discover what opportunity there might be to escape. But the wiser Joe Hawkridge counseled patience, saying:

"Wait a bit. We'd be as helpless as any babes should we take to our heels in this ungodly wilderness. Is there a town or plantation near by?"

"I know not," ruefully confessed Jack. "Charles Town lies to the south, and Virginia to the north. There my knowledge fetches up short."

"And leagues of morass to flounder through, by the look of this coast," said Joe. "We be without weapons, or food, or——"

"I am a hot-headed fool, I grant you that," broke in Jack. "Now bestow your sage advice."

"You will not be allowed to go ashore, for one thing, Master Cockrell. Blackbeard has no notion of letting you get away from him to betray this rendezvous and stir the colonies to send an expedition after him. Steadythe helm, Jack, and watch for squalls. If I can read the signs, there is trouble afoot. And we must seek our own advantage in the nick of time."

"But these wild sots no longer think of mutiny and the like, Joe. They are content to let the morrow go hang."

"S-s-s-h, 'ware the master of the sloop," cautioned Joe. "He makes for the gangway, the big lump of tallow."

They moved away while Captain Richard Spender clumsily descended into his boat, his broad face flushed, his breath asthmatic. He had a piping voice absurd for his bulk and the two lads amused themselves with mimicking him as the boat pulled in the direction of the sloop. So safe against surprise did Blackbeard regard himself in this lonely anchorage that no more than a dozen men were left aboard to keep the ship through the night. Among these was Jack Cockrell, as his comrade had foreseen. It therefore happened that they remained together, for Joe had volunteered to join the anchor watch. In a melancholy mood the two lads idled upon the after deck.

The sun dropped behind the dark and tangled forest and flights of herons came winging it home to the islets in the swamps. On the sward by the silver strand the throng of pirates had stilled their clamor while a rascal with a tenor voice held them enraptured with the haunting refrain of:

"Sweet Annie frae the sea-beach came,
Where Jockey's climbed the vessel's side:
Ah! wha can keep her heart at hame,
When Jockey's tossed aboon the tide?

"Far off 'till distant realms he gangs,
But I'se be true, as he ha' been;
And when ilk lass around him thrangs,
He'll think on Annie's faithful een."

Forlorn Jack Cockrell had homesick thoughts and felt hopeless of loosing the snares which bound him. All that sustained his courage was the sanguine disposition of Joe Hawkridge, whose youthful soul had been so battered and toughened by dangers manifold on land and sea that he expected nothing less. Listening to the pirate's moving ballad, they sat and swung their legs from the ship's taffrail while their gaze idly roved to the green curtain of undergrowth which ran lush to the water's edge to the northward of the beach.

It was Joe who called attention to a floating object which moved inside the mouth of the small, tidal creek that wandered through the marshy lowlands. In the shadowy light it could easily be mistaken for a log drifting down on the ebb of the tide. This was what the lads assumed it to be until they both noticed a behavior curious in a log. The long, low object turned athwart the current at the entrance of the creek and shot toward the nearest bank as though strongly propelled.

Joe lifted the telescope from its case in front of the wooden binnacle-box and squinted long at the edge of the creek. Crude though the glass was, he was enabled to discern that the object was, in truth, a log, but evidently hollowed out. Rounded at the ends, it held two men whose figures so blended into the dusk that they disclosed themselves only when in motion.

"A pirogue," said Joe, "and fashioned by Indians! What is the tribe hereabouts? Have ye a guess?"

"Roving Yemassees, or men of the Hatteras tribe," answered Jack. "Yonder brace of savages will be scouts."

"Aye, but there'll be no attack 'gainst this pirates' bivouac, right under the guns of the ships. The Indians are too wise to attempt it."

"Look, Joe! Hand me the glass. Those two spies have quitted the pirogue. 'Tis quite empty. They may lay up all night to creep closer and keep watch on the camp."

"Right enough, by Crambo! If we could but gain yon cypress canoe, and steal along the coast by sail and paddle——"

"'Tis the chance we prayed for," eagerly exclaimed Jack. "Dare we swim for it?"

"Not with a boat just coming off from shore. What if we try it in the night and find the pirogue gone?"

"We are stranded for sure, and Blackbeard will kill us."

Baffled, they strained their eyes until the shore stood black in the starlight, but as long as the dusk lingered they fancied they could descry the empty pirogue. The ship's boat which presently drew alongside contained Blackbeard himself and Captain Dick Spender of the *Triumph* sloop, besides several officers of the two vessels. They withdrew into the cabin and there was prolonged discussion, lasting well toward midnight.

It was a secretive session, with trusted men of the boat's crew posted to keep eavesdroppers away from the hatches and windows, nor was there any loud carousing. Some business was afoot and Jack wondered whether it might concern the trouble which Joe had sworn was brewing under the surface. A circumstance even more suspicious was that three of the sailors from the boat were called into the cabin. Joe Hawkridge knew them as fellows loyal to Blackbeard through thick and thin. Drunken beasts, as a rule, they were cold sober to-night.

As quietly as they had come, the whole party dropped into the boat and returned either to the beach or to the sloop which rode at anchor two cable-lengths away. The *Revenge* floated with no more activity on her darkened decks. The few men of the watch drowsed at their stations or wistfully gazed at the fires ashore and the mob of pirates who moved in the red glare. Jack Cockrell and Joe Hawkridge felt no desire for sleep. As the ship swung with the turn of the tide, they went to the side and leaned on the tall bulwark where they mightcatch the first glimpse of the shore with the break of day.

Meanwhile they busied themselves with this wild scheme and that. Sifting them out, it was resolved to swim from the ship at the first opportunity. If they could not find the Indian pirogue, Joe would try to get into the pirates' camp by night and possess himself of an axe, an adze, a musket or two, and such food as he could smuggle out. Then, at a pinch, they could hide themselves a little way inland and hew out a pirogue of their own from a dry log. After hitting upon this plan, the better it seemed the more they thrashed it over.

Unluckily it occurred to them so late in the night that they feared to attempt it then lest the dawn might overtake them while they were swimming. 'Twas a great pity, said Joe, that their wits had hung fire, like a damp flint-lock, for this was the night when the pirates would be the most slack and befuddled and it would be precious hard waiting through another day. Jack glumly agreed with this point of view.

It was so near morning, however, that they lingered to scan the shore. Then it was observed that a pearly mist was rising from the swamp lands and spreading out over the water. It was almost like a fog which the morning breeze would dispel after a while. Rolling like smoke it hung so low that the topmast of the sloop rose above it although her hull was like the gray ghost of a vessel

"No sign of wind as yet," said Joe, holding up a wetted finger, "and that red sunset bespoke a calm, hot day. This odd smother o' mist may stay a couple of hours. Will ye venture it with me, Jack?"

"Gladly! Over we go, before the watch is flogged awake by the bos'n's mate."

They crept aft to the high stern and paid out a coil of rope until it trailed in the water beneath the railed gallery which overhung the huge rudder. Joe belayed his end securely and slid over like a flash, twisting the rope around one leg and letting himself down as agile as a monkey. Without a splash he cast himself loose and Jack followed but not so adroitly. When he plopped into the water the commotion was like tossing a barrel overboard, but nobody sounded an alarm.

They clung to the rusty rudder chains and listened. The ship was all quiet. Then out into the mist they launched themselves, swimming almost submerged, dreading to hear an outcry and the spatter of musket balls. But the veiling mist and the uncertain light of dawn soon protected the fugitives. It was slow, exhausting progress, hampered as they were by their breeches and shoes which could not be discarded. They tried to keep a sense of direction, striking out for the mouth of the creek in which the pirogue had been moored, but the tide set them off the course and the only visible marks were the spars of the ship behind them and the sloop's topmast off to one side

Jack swam more strongly and showed greater endurance because he had the beef and had been better nourished all his life than the scrawny young powder boy who was more like a lath. Now and then Jack paused to tread water while his shipmate clung to his shoulder and husbanded his waning strength, with that indomitable grin on his freckled phiz. Of one thing they were thankful, that the tide was bearing them farther away from the pirates' camp, which was now as still as though the sleepers were dead men.

"Blood and bones, but I have swum a league a'ready," gurgled Joe during one of the halts.

"Shut your mouth or you'll fill up to the hatch and founder," scolded Jack. "I see trees in the mist. The shore is scarce a pistol shot away."

"I pray my keel scrapes soon," spluttered the waterlogged Hawkridge as he kicked himself along in a final effort.

Huzza, their feet touched the soft ooze and they fell over stumps and rotted trunks buried under the surface. Scratched and beplastered with mud, they crawled out in muck which gripped them to the knees, and roosted like buzzards upon the butt of a prostrate live-oak.

"Marooned," quoth Joe, "to be eaten by snakes and alligators."

"Nonsense," snapped Master Cockrell, who had hunted deer and wild-fowl on the Carolina coast. "Wecan pick our way with care. I have seen pleasanter landscapes than this, but I like it better than Blackbeard's company."

JACK ALMOST BUMPED INTO THE DUGOUT CANOE

There was no disputing this statement and Joe plucked up spirit, as was his habit when another arduous task confronted him. Cautiously they made their way from one quaking patch of sedge to another or scrambled to their middles. There came a ridge of higher ground thick with brambles and knotted vines and they traversed this with less misery. A gleam of water among the trees and they took it to be the creek which they sought to find. Wary of lurking Indians, they wormed along on their stomachs and so came to the high swamp grass of the bank.

They swam the creek and crept toward its mouth. Jack was rooting along like a bear when he almost bumped into the dugout canoe which had looked so very like a stranded log. It was tied to a tree by a line of twisted fibre and the rising tide had borne it well up into the marsh. Here it was invisible from the ship and only a miracle of good fortune had revealed it to the lads in that glimpse from the deck at sundown.

They crawled over the gunwale and slumped in the bottom of the pirogue, which was larger than they expected, a clumsy yet seaworthy craft with a wide floor and space to crowd a dozen men. Fire had helped to hollow it from a giant of a cypress log, for the inner skin was charred black. Three roughly made paddleswere discovered. This was tremendously important, and all they lacked was a mast and sail to be true navigators.

Something else they presently found which was so unlooked for, so incredible, that they could only gape and stare at each other. Tucked in the bow was a seaman's jacket of tarred canvas, of the kind used in wet weather. Sewed to the inside of it was a pocket of leather with a buttoned flap. This Jack Cockrell proceeded to explore, recovering from his stupefaction, and fished out a wallet bound in sharkskin as was the habit of sailors to make for themselves in tropic waters. It contained nothing of value, a few scraps of paper stitched together, a bit of coral, a lock of yellow hair, a Spanish coin, some shreds of dried tobacco leaf.

Carefully Jack examined the ragged sheets of paper which seemed to be a carelessly jotted diary of dates and events. Upon the last leaf was scrawled, *"Bill Saxby, His Share,"* and beneath this entry such items as these:

"Aprl. ye 17—A Spanish shippe rich laden. 1 sack Vanilla. 2 Rolls Blue Cloth of Peru. 1 Packet Bezoar Stones.

"May ye 24—A Poor Shippe. 3 Bars of Silver. 1 Case Cordial Waters. A Golden Candle-stick. My share by Lot afore ye Mast."

Joe Hawkridge could neither read nor write but he had ready knowledge of the meaning of these entries and he cried excitedly:

"Say the name again, Jack. Bill Saxby, His Share. Strike me blind, but I was chums with Bill when we lay off Honduras. As decent a lad as ever went a-piratin'! A heart of oak is Bill, hailin' from London town."

"But what of the riddle?" impatiently demanded Jack. "Whence this Indian pirogue? And where is Bill Saxby?"

"He sailed with Stede Bonnet, bless ye," answered Joe. "These two men we spied in the canoe last night were no Indians. *They were Cap'n Bonnet's men.* Indians would ha' hid the pirogue more craftily."

"But they came not along the coast. Did they drop down this creek from somewhere inland?"

"There you put me in stays," confessed Joe. "One thing I can swear. They were sent to look for Blackbeard's ships. And I sore mistrust they were caught whilst prowling near the camp. Else they would ha' come back to the canoe before day."

CHAPTER VIII

THE EPISODE OF THE WINDING CREEK

THE singular discovery of Bill Saxby's jacket was like a shock to drive all else out of their minds. Now they found that it had been thrown over a jug of water and a bag of beef and biscuit stowed in the bow. This solved one pressing problem, and they nibbled the hard ration while debating the situation. It was agreed that they could not honorably run away with the pirogue if it really belonged to Stede Bonnet's men, who must have come on foot along the higher ground back of the coast and descended the creek in the canoe stolen or purchased from Indians met by chance.

Granted this much, it was fair to conjecture that Captain Bonnet's ship was in some harbor not many leagues distant and that he knew where to find Blackbeard's rendezvous, at Cherokee Inlet.

"'Tis your job to stand by the pirogue, Jack," suggested Hawkridge, "and I will make a sally toward the pirates' camp afore they rouse out."

"Go softly, Joe, and don't be reckless. Why not lie up till night before you reconnoitre?"

"'Cause the mist still hangs heavy and I'm blowed if I dilly-dally if good Bill Saxby has come to grief."

"Supposing he has, you cannot wrest him single-handed from Blackbeard's crew."

"Well, if I can but slip a word of comfort in his ear, it'll cheer him mightily, unless his throat be cut by now," was the stubborn response. "Sit thee taut, Jack, old *camarada*, and chuck the worry. Care killed a cat. These rogues yonder in the camp won't *molest me* if I walk boldly amongst 'em."

"What if you don't return?" persisted Jack. "How long shall I wait here with the pirogue?"

"Now what the deuce can I say to such foolish queries? If things go wrong with me and Bill and his mate, you will have to cruise alone or hop back to the *Revenge*."

With a laugh and a wave of the hand, the dauntless adventurer leaped from the nose of the canoe, nimbly hauled himself into a tree, and then plunged into the gloomy swamp where he was speedily lost to view. Jack Cockrell settled himself to wait for he knew not what. Clouds of midges and mosquitoes tormented him and he ached with fatigue. Soon after sunrise the mist began to burn away and the mouth of the creek was no longer obscured by shadows. In the glare of day Jack thought it likely that the canoe might be detected by some pair of keen eyes aboard the *Revenge*.

To move it far might imperil Joe Hawkridge and Bonnet's two seamen should they come in haste with a hue-and-cry behind them. Jack paddled the pirogue up the creek and soon found a safe ambuscade, a stagnant cove in among the dense growth, where he tied up to a gnarled root. Then he climbed a wide-branching oak and propped himself in a crotch from which he could see the open water and the two vessels at anchor. Clumps of taller trees cut off any view of the beach and the camp but he dared stray no farther from the pirogue.

Tediously an hour passed and there was no sign of Joe Hawkridge. He had a journey of only a few hundred yards to make, and Jack began to imagine all kinds of misfortune that might have befallen him, such as being mired beyond his depth in the swamp and perishing miserably. The sensible conclusion was, however, that he had tarried among his shipmates in the camp with some shrewd purpose in mind.

A little later in the morning, Jack's anxious cogitations were diverted by the frequent passage of boats between the *Revenge* and the sloop which was anchored nearer the beach. One of these small craft was Blackbeard's own cock-boat, or captain's gig, which he used for errands in smooth water, with a couple of men to pull it. Jack was reminded of that secret conference in the cabin and Joe's conviction that some uncommon devilment was afoot. It appeared as though "Tallow Dick" Spender, that unwholesome master of the *Triumph* sloop, had been chosen as the right bower.

And now there arose a sudden and riotous noise in the camp. It was not the mirth and song of jolly pirates a-pleasuring ashore but the ferocious tumult of men in conflict and taken unawares. Perched in the tree, Jack Cockrell listened all agog as the sounds rose and fell with the breeze which swayed the long gray moss that draped the branches. He heard a few pistol shots and then was startled to see a spurt of flame dart from a gun-port of the sloop. The dull report reached him an instant later. He could see that the gun had been fired from the vessel's shoreward battery. It meant that Blackbeard was making a target of some part of the camp. Another gun belched its cloud of smoke.

The noise died down, save for intermittent shouts and one long wail of anguish. Presently a boat moved out past the sloop. A dozen men tugged at the oars and others stood crowded in the stern-sheets. Jack caught the gleam of weapons and thought he recognized the squat, broad figure of Blackbeard himself beside the man at the steering oar. Behind this pinnace from the *Revenge* trailed two other boats in tow.

They passed in slow procession, out between the vessels. The boats which the pinnace towed were not empty. Instead of sitting upon the thwarts, men seemed to be strewn about in them as if they had been tossed over the gunwales like so much dunnage.

Jack rubbed his eyes in amazement and watched the line of boats turn to follow the channel which led out of the sheltered roadstead to the sea beyond. When they vanished beyond a sandy island, the lad in the live-oak tree said to himself:

"My guess is that Blackbeard has put a stopper on all talk of mutiny by one bold stroke. A bloody weeding-out, and in those two boats are the poor wretches who were taken alive. Alas, one of 'em may be Joe Hawkridge unless he be dead already. He talked too much of Stede Bonnet aboard the ship. And there were sneaking dogs in the crew who spied on their comrades. We saw them enter the cabin last night."

There was no getting around the evidence. It fitted together all too well. Jack sadly reflected that, beyond a doubt, he had seen the last of gallant, loyal Joe Hawkridge. Left alone with the pirogue, which he could not paddle single-handed, it was folly to think of trying to escape along the coast. And to wander inland, ignorant of the country, was to court almost certain death. Nor could he now expect mercy from Blackbeard, having deserted the ship against orders and known to be a true friend of Captain Stede Bonnet.

The most unhappy lad could no longer hold his cramped station in the tree and he decided to seek the canoe and find the meagre solace of a little food and water. He was half-way to the ground when he clutched a limb and halted to peer into the swamp. Something was splashing through the mud and grass and making a prodigious fuss about it.

Then Jack heard two voices in grunts and maledictions. Fearing the enemy might have tracked him, he stood as still as a mouse in the leafage of the oak.

Out of the swamp emerged a young man with a musket on his shoulder. Behind him came one very much older, gaunt and wrinkled, his hair as gray as the Spanish moss that overhung his path. They reached the edge of the creek and then turned down to halt where the pirogue had been left. At failing to find it there, they argued hotly and were much distressed. Jack Cockrell's fears were calmed. These were no men of Blackbeard's company, but good Bill Saxby and his mate. He called to them from his perch and they stood wondering at this voice from heaven.

In a jiffy Jack had slid down and was beckoning them. They hurried as fast as they could pull their feet out of the muck, and were overjoyed to jump into the hidden canoe. There they sat and thumped Jack Cockrell on the head by way of affectionate greeting. The younger man had a chubby cheek, a dimple in his chin, and blue eyes as big and round as a babe's.

"Bill Saxby is me," said his pleasant voice, "and a precious job had I to get here. Joe Hawkridge told me of you, Master Cockrell."

"Where is Joe?" cried Jack, dreading to hear his own opinion confirmed.

"Marooned, along with two dozen luckless lads that were trapped like pigeons——"

"'Twas more like turtles all a-sleepin' in the sand," the old man croaked in rusty accents. "A few was sharp awake and they fought pretty whilst the rest rallied, but they got drove with their backs to the swamp and a deep slough. Then the sloop turned her guns on 'em and they struck their colors."

"And Joe Hawkridge sided with his friends, of course," said Jack.

"Would ye expect aught else of him?" proudly answered Bill Saxby. "He searched us out where we lay trussed like fowls, all bound with ropes. We blundered fair into the camp last night, and old Trimble Rogers here, his legs knotted with cramps, couldn't make a run for it. They saved us for Blackbeard's pleasure but he had other fish to fry."

"What then?" demanded Jack.

"'Twas Joe Hawkridge that ran to cut our bonds when the fight began. And he bade us leg it for the pirogue and carry word to you. A pledge of honor, he called it, to stand by his dear friend Jack, and he made us swear it."

"Bless him for a Christian knight of a pirate," said Jack, with tears in his eyes. "Was he hurt, did ye happen to note?"

"We hid ourselves till the prisoners were flung into the boats. I marked Joe as one of 'em, and he was sprightly, barring a bloody face."

"Marooned, Bill Saxby?" asked Jack. "What's your judgment on that score? It cannot be many leagues from here, or the ship would have transported them instead of the boats."

"These barren islands lie strung well out from the coast, Master Cockrell. Waterless they be, and without shelter. Blackbeard's fancy is to let the men die there——"

"An ancient custom of buccaneers and pirates," put in old Trimble Rogers, with an air of grave authority. "I mind me in the year of 1687 when I sailed in the South Sea with that great captain, Edward Davis,—'twas after the sack of Guayaquil when every man had a greater weight of gold and silver than he could lug on his back——"

Bill Saxby interrupted, in a petulant manner:

"Stow it, grandsire! At a better time ye can please the lad with your long-winded yarns,—of marching on Panama with Henry Morgan when the mother's milk was scarce dry on your lips."

"I cruised with the best of 'em," boasted the last of the storied race of true buccaneers of the Spanish Main, "and now I be in this cheap trade of piratin'. The fortunes I gamed away, and the plate ships I boarded! Take warnin', boy, and salt your treasure down."

"This Trimble Rogers will talk you deaf," said Bill Saxby, "but there's pith in his old bones and wisdom under yon hoary thatch. Cap'n Bonnet sent him along with me as a rare old hound to trail the swamps."

In a vivid flash of remembrance, Jack Cockrell saw this salty relic of the Spanish Main among the crew which had disported itself on the tavern green at Charles Town,—the old man sitting aside with a couple of stray children upon his knees while his head nodded to the lilt of the fiddle. And again there had been a glimpse of him trudging in the column which had followed Stede Bonnet, with trumpet and drum, to attack the hostile Indians. Jack's heart warmed to Trimble Rogers and also to young Bill Saxby. They would find some way out of all this tribulation.

"Whither lies Captain Bonnet's stout ship?" eagerly demanded Jack.

"On this side the Western Ocean," smiled Saxby. "We shall waste no time in finding her. We had better bide where we are a few hours, eh, Trimble?"

"Aye, and double back up the stream in the canoe to spend the night on dry land and push on afoot at dawn. If we wait to sight Blackbeard's boats come in from sea, 'twill aid us to reckon how far out they went and what the bearings are."

"So Captain Bonnet may sail to pick off those poor seamen marooned," exclaimed Jack.

"He is not apt to leave 'em to bleach their bones," said Bill Saxby. "And when it comes to closing in with Blackbeard, they will have a grudge of their own."

They made themselves as comfortable as possible on the bottom of the pirogue. Now and then Jack climbed the live-oak to look for the return of the boats. There was no more leisure for the pirates left in the ship and the sloop. Evidently Blackbeard had been alarmed by the tidings that two of Stede Bonnet's men had been caught spying him out and had made their escape in the confusion. The sloop was now listed over in shoal water and Bill Saxby ventured the opinion that they intended to take the mast out of her and put it in the *Revenge*.

"Along with most of her guns, I take it," said Trimble Rogers. "What with losing all those men, in one way or another, this Blackbeard, as Cap'n Ed'ard Teach miscalls hisself, must needs abandon the sloop. The more the merrier, says I, when we come at close quarters."

Jack asked many curious questions, by way of passing the time. The old man was easy to read. He had been a lawless sea rover in the days when there was both gold and glory in harrying Spanish towns and galleons, from Mexico to Peru. The real buccaneers had vanished but he was too old a dog to learn new tricks and he faithfully served Stede Bonnet, who had a spark of the chivalry and manliness which had burned so brightly in that idolized master, Captain Edward Davis.

As for this blue-eyed smiling young Bill Saxby, he had been a small tradesman in London. Through no fault of his own, he was cruelly imprisoned for debt and, after two years, shipped to the Carolina plantations as no better than a slave. For all he knew, the girl wifeand child in London had been suffered to starve. He had never heard any word of them. As a fugitive he had been taken aboard a pirate vessel. There he found kindlier treatment than honest men had ever offered him, and so grew somewhat reconciled to this wicked calling.

On one of the occasions when Jack left these entertaining companions to visit his high sentry post in the tree, he surmised that all hands had been summoned on the vessel and lifting out her mast. He could see two boats plying back and forth and filled with men. He lingered because something else caught his interest. A little boat was putting out from the seaward side of the *Revenge* and it fetched a wide circuit of the harbor. This brought the ship between it and the sloop so that its departure would be unobserved by the toiling crew.

Two men were at the oars and a third sat in the stern. At a distance, Jack guessed they were bound to one of the nearest islands, perhaps in search of oysters or crabs, but after making a long sweep which carried the boat out of vision of the sloop and the beach, it swung toward the shore, a little to the northward of the mouth of the creek. The errand had a stealthy air. Jack Cockrell started and almost fell out of the tree. He had been mistaken in his fancy that Blackbeard was in the pinnace which had towed the prisoners out to be marooned. This was none other than the grotesque fiend of a pirate himself, furtively steering his cock-boat on some private errand of his own.

As soon as he was certain of this, Jack fairly scurried down the tree, digging his toes in the bark like a squirrel, and tumbling head over heels into the pirogue. Breathing rapidly, he stuttered:

"The—the devil himself,—in that little w-wherry of his,—c-coming inshore. He must ha' seen the canoe. He is in chase of me."

"Go take a look, Bill," coolly remarked old Trimble Rogers, who was busy slapping at mosquitoes. "A touch o' the sun has bred a nightmare in the lad."

Bill Saxby swarmed up the live-oak like a limber seaman with fish-hooks for fingers and he, too, almost lost his balance at what he saw. He waved a warning hand at the canoe and then put his fingers to his lips. Down he came in breakneck haste and urged the others to haul their craft farther up into the sedge. He was plucking green bushes and armfuls of dried grass to fling across the gunwales.

Satisfied that the canoe was entirely concealed, they crouched low. The old man was more concerned with the pest of insects and he reached out to claw up the sticky mud with which he plastered his face and neck like a mask. This seemed to give him some relief and his comrades were glad to do the same. Bill Saxby was attentive to the priming of the musket, which he passed over to Trimble Rogers, saying:

"You are the chief gunner, old hawk. But hold your fire. I'm itching to know what trick this Don Whiskerando is up to."

"Fair enough," muttered the old man. "Cap'n Bonnet 'ud clap me in irons if I slew this filthy Ed'ard Teach and robbed him of that enjoyment. I'll pull no trigger save in our own defense."

They heard the faint splash of oars. Soon the little cock-boat came gliding around the bend of the shore and floated into the mouth of the creek. Bill Saxby raised himself for a moment and ducked swiftly as he whispered:

"He is not lookin' about but motions 'em to row on up the stream."

"Then our canoe is not what he's after?" murmured Jack.

"'Tis some queer game. Were he hunting us, he'd fetch along more hands than them two. Hush! Let him pass."

The little boat came steadily on, the tide helping the oars. It sat very low in the water, oddly so for the weight of three men. Blackbeard, hunched in the stern, held a pistol in one hand while the other gripped the tiller. This was not in fear of danger from the shore because he kept his eyes on the two seamen at the oars and it was plain to see that the pistol was meant to menace them.

The boat passed abreast of the pirogue so artfullyconcealed in the pocket of a tiny cove. The intervening distance was no more than a dozen yards. Old Trimble Rogers wistfully fingered the musket and lifted it to squint along the barrel. Never was temptation more sturdily resisted. Then his face, hard as iron and puckered like dried leather, broke into a smile. The idea pleased him immensely. They would follow Blackbeard and watch the chance to take him alive. He who had trapped his own men in camp was now neatly trapped himself, his retreat cut off. Tie a couple of fathom of stout cord to his whiskers and tow him along by land, all the way to Stede Bonnet's ship. There the worthy captain could bargain with him at his own terms, silently chuckled the old buccaneer.

They held their breath and gazed at the fantastic scoundrel who had made himself the ogre among pirates. He had discarded the great hat as cumbersome and his tousled head was bound around with a wide strip of the red calico from India. Still and solid he sat, like a heathen idol, staring in front of him and intent on his mysterious errand. The unseen spectators in the pirogue scanned also the two seamen at the oars and felt a vague pity for them. Unmistakably they were sick with fear. It was conveyed by their dejected aspect, by the tinge of pallor, by the fixity with which they regarded the cocked pistol in Blackbeard's fist. Jack Cockrell knew them as abandoned villains who had boasted of many a bloody deed but the swarthy, pockmarked fellow had been in the boat which had saved the two lads from the drifting raft. This was enough to awaken a lively sympathy.

Trimble Rogers gripped Jack's shoulder with a strength which made him wince and pointed a skinny finger at the boat. The fate of the two seamen did not trouble him greatly. Those who lived by violence should rightly expect to die by it. The sea was their gaming table and it was their ill luck if the dice were cogged. Just then Bill Saxby stifled an ejaculation. He, too, had discovered the freightage in the cock-boat, the heavy burden which made it swim so low.

It rested in front of Blackbeard's knees, the top showing above the curve of the gunwales. It was a sea-chest, uncommonly large, built of some dark tropical wood and strapped with iron. Old Trimble Rogers' fierce eyes glittered and he licked his lips. He leaned over to whisper in Bill Saxby's ear the one word:

"Treasure!"

CHAPTER IX

BLACKBEARD'S ERRAND IS INTERRUPTED

BLACKBEARD'S deep-laden boat was rowed on past the pirogue and turned to follow the channel of the sluggish stream. Bill Saxby thrust aside the cover of grass and boughs and shoved the log canoe out of the cove. So crooked was the course of the creek that the boat was already out of sight and by stealthy paddling it was possible to pursue undetected. Old Trimble Rogers had forgotten his lust to slay Blackbeard. His gloating imagination could picture the contents of that massive sea-chest after a long cruise in southern waters.

It was foolish to attempt to surprise Blackbeard while afloat in the creek. In a race of it, the handy cock-boat could pull away from the clumsier pirogue manned by two paddles only, for Trimble Rogers was needed to steer and be ready with the musket. This was their only firearm, which Bill Saxby had snatched up during the flight from the camp. At the same time he had lifted a powder-horn and bullet pouch from a wounded pirate.

"If I do bang away and miss him," grumbled Trimble Rogers, "he's apt to pepper us afore I can reload

"But you forswore shootin' him," chided Bill Saxby, between strokes of the paddle.

"Show me a great sea-chest crammed wi' treasure and I'd put a hole through the Grand High Panjandrum hisself," replied the ancient one. "Aye, Bill, there be more'n one way to skin an eel. We'll lay aboard this bloody blow-hard of a Cap'n Teach whilst he's a-buryin' of it. Here may well be where he has tucked away his other plunder. What if we bag the whole of it?"

"One more fling, eh, Trimble, and more gold than ye lugged on your back from Guayaquil," grinned young Bill.

They had spoken in cautious tones and now held their tongues. The paddles dipped with no more than a trickle of water and the canoe hugged the marsh. They were close to the next bend of the stream and the sound of the oars in the cock-boat was faintly audible. As the tallest of the three, the old man stood up after swathing his head in dried grass, and gazed across the curve of the shore. By signs he told his companions that Blackbeard was bound farther up the stream.

They waited a little, giving their quarry time to pass beyond another turn of the channel. Jack Cockrell was embarked on the most entrancing excursion of his life. This repaid him for all he had suffered. His only regret was that poor Joe Hawkridge had been marooned before he could share this golden adventure. However, he would see that Joe received a handsome amount of treasure. Trimble Rogers was muttering again, and thus he angrily expounded a grievance:

"A thief is this Cap'n Teach,—like a wild hog, all greed and bristles. 'Tis the custom of honest buccaneers and pirates to divide the spoils by the strict rule,—six shares for the commander, two for the master's mate, and other officers accordin' to their employment, with one share to every seaman alike. Think ye this bloody pick-purse dealt fairly by his crew? In yon sea-chest be the lawful shares of all the woesome lads he marooned this day. An' as much more as he durst skulk away with."

"Easy, now, old Fire-and-Brimstone," warned Bill, "or that temper will gain the upper hand. Don't spoil the show by bombardin' Blackbeard with that cross-eyed musket."

Now here was young Master Cockrell, a gentleman and a near kinsman of a high official who had sworn to hang every mother's son of a pirate that harried Carolina waters. And yet this godly youth was eager to lay hands on Blackbeard's treasure so as to divide it among the pirates who had been robbed of it. It was a twisted sense of justice, no doubt, and a code of morals turned topsy-turvy, but you are entreated to think not too harshly of such behavior. Master Cockrell had fallen into almighty bad company but the friends he had made displayed fidelity and readiness to serve him.

"How far will the chase lead us?" he inquired.

"Did you men come down this same creek in the pirogue?"

"Aye, in this very same mess o' pea soup and jungle," answered Bill Saxby. "Two miles in from the coast, at a venture, was where we stumbled on the canoe and tossed the Indians out of it. Beyond that the water spreads o'er the swamp with no fairway for a boat."

Once more they paddled for a short stretch and then repeated the stratagem of hauling into the dense growth of the mud-flat and pausing until the cock-boat had steered beyond the next elbow of the stream. It became more and more difficult to avoid the fallen trees and other obstructions, but Blackbeard was threading his course like a pilot acquainted with this dank and somber region. The pirogue ceased to lag purposely but had to be urged in order to keep within striking distance.

Twice they were compelled to climb out and shove clear of sunken entanglements or slimy shoals. But when they held themselves to listen, they could still hear the measured thump of oars against the pins, like the beat of a distant drum in the brooding silence of this melancholy solitude. They had struggled on for perhaps a mile and a half, in all, when Trimble Rogers ordered another halt. He was perplexed, like a hound uncertain of the scent. From the left bank of the creek, a smaller stream meandered blindly off into the swamp. Into which of these watercourses had Blackbeard continued his secret voyage?

Again they listened, and more anxiously than ever. The tell-tale thump of the oars had ceased. The only sounds in the bayou were the trickle of water from the tidal pools, the wind in the tree-tops, the rat-tat-tat of a woodpecker, and the scream of a bob-cat. With a foolish air of chagrin, Trimble Rogers rubbed his hoary pate and exclaimed:

"Whilst Bill and me were a-paddlin' this hollow log down-stream, we took no heed of a fork like this yonder. With the sun at our backs to guide us, we knew we was makin' easterly to fetch the coast. What say, Bill?"

"Cursed if I know. Spin a coin. The treasure has slipped us."

"Rot me if it has!" snarled the old man. "We'll push on as we are, in the bigger stream. That stinkin' ditch on my left hand looks too weedy and shallow to float a boat."

"It makes no odds. A gamester's choice," amiably agreed Bill.

They paddled with might and main, flinging caution to the winds. Jack Cockrell was well versed in handling one of these dugout canoes and his stout arms made Bill Saxby grunt and sweat to keep stroke with him. When the craft grounded they strove like madmen to push it clear. Trimble Rogers tore the water with a paddle, straining every sinew and condemning Blackbeard to the bottomless pit in a queer jargon of the Spanish, French, and English tongues. It required such a lurid vocabulary to give vent to his feelings. He was even more distressed when he sighted the clump of gum trees near by which he and Bill had purloined the pirogue. Beyond this the creek was impassable.

"Throwed a blank! Wear ship and drive back to the fork o' the waters," shouted the old man. "Hull down an' under though he be, we'll nab yon *picaro*, with his jolly treasure. *Rapido, camaradas! Vivo!*"

To make haste was easier said than done but the sluggish current was now in their favor and there was no more than a half mile to traverse under stress of furious exertion. The heavy canoe crashed through obstacles which had delayed the upward journey and they knew where to avoid the worst of the shoals. What fretted them was the fear that Blackbeard might have buried the sea-chest and descended the creek while they were engaged in this wild-goose chase. But this seemed unlikely and, moreover, old Trimble Rogers was the man to nose out the marks of the landing-place and the trail which must have been left.

Where the two streams joined, the pirogue turned and shot into the smaller one. To their surprise it presently widened and was like a tiny lagoon, with the water much clearer as if fed by springs. The view was less broken and there were glimpses of dry knolls in the swamp and verdure not so noxious and tanglesome. Along the edge of this pretty pond skimmed the pirogue while Trimble Rogers keenly scanned every inch of it for the imprint of a boat's keel. A hundred yards and the water again narrowed to a little creek. Impetuously the canoe swung to pass around a spit of land covered with a thicket of sweet bay.

There, no more than a dozen feet beyond, was the captain's cock-boat from the *Revenge*. Its bow had been pulled out of the water which deepened from a shelving bank. The boat was deserted but above the gunwale could be seen the iron-bound lid of the massive sea-chest. Those in the pirogue desired to behold nothing else. They were suddenly diverted by a tremendous yell which came booming out of the tall grass where it waved breast-high on the shore of the stream. A pistol barked and the ball clipped a straggling lock of Trimble Rogers' gray hair.

Driving his two seamen before him, Blackbeard rushed for his boat as fast as the bandy legs and clumsy sea-boots could carry him. In fancied security he had explored the nearest knoll. And now appeared this infernal canoe, surging full-tilt at his treasure chest.

Things happened *rapido* enough to glut even an old buccaneer. The consternation in the pirogue prevented any thought of checking headway with the paddles. This hollowed cypress log, narrow beamed and solid at both ends, still moved with a weighty momentum. Its astounded crew were otherwise occupied. Blackbeard appeared to have the advantage of them. Jack Cockrell ducked to the bottom of the canoe. Bill Saxby's eyes of baby blue were big and round as saucers as he wildly flourished his paddle as the only cudgel at hand.

With a whoop-la, old Trimble Rogers leaped to his feet, the long musket at his shoulder. Before he could aim at the savage, bushy figure of Blackbeard, the prow of the pirogue crashed into the side of the cock-boat, striking it well toward the stern. The ancient freebooter described a somersault and smote the water with a mighty splash, musket and all. Blowing like a grampus, he bobbed to the top, clawing the weeds from his eyes but still clutching the musket. Nobody paid his misfortune the slightest heed.

The water deepened suddenly, as has been said, where the current had scoured the bank. With the nose of the little boat pulled well up in the mud, the stern sloped almost level with the surface of the stream. The blunt, slanting bow of the pirogue banged into the plank gunwale and slid over it. The force of the blow dragged the cock-boat to one side and wrenched it free of the shore. It floated at the end of a tether but the bow of the canoe pressed the stern under and tipped it until the water rushed in.

Listed far over, the sea-chest slid a trifle and this was enough to push the gunwale clear under. The boat filled and capsized, what with the weight of the chest and the pressure of the canoe's fore part. Down to the oozy bed sank Blackbeard's treasure.

The arch-pirate himself came charging out of the marsh-grass in time to witness this lamentable disaster. His hoarse ejaculations were too dreadful for a Christian reader's ears. Dumfounded for an instant, he gathered his wits to fire another pistol at the pirogue. The ball flew wild, as was to be expected of a marksman in a state of mind so distraught. He had overlooked those two poor seamen of his who had been impressed to bury the treasure, after which they were presumably to be pistoled or knocked on the head. Dead men told no tales. Doomed wretches, they were quick to snatch from this confusion the precious hope of life.

The pockmarked fellow, who was powerfully built, whirled like a cat as he heard Blackbeard's pistol discharged just behind him. There was no time to draw and cock another pistol. The seaman fairly flew at the pirate captain's throat. Down they toppled and vanished in the grass together. A moment later Blackbeard bounded to his feet, a bloody dirk in his hand. He had done for the poor fellow who lay groaning where he fell. Terrified by this, the other seaman wheeled and fled to the bank of the creek, seeking the pirogue as his only refuge.

He leaped for it but his feet slipped in the treacherous mud and his impetus was checked so that he tumbled forward, striking the solid side of the dugout with great force. He was splashing in the water but his exertions were feeble. Either the collision had stunned him or he was unable to swim. Bill Saxby and Jack Cockrell were trying to swing the canoe clear of the boat and effect a landing. Trimble Rogers had rescued himself from the creek and was ramming a dry charge into his dripping musket. Blackbeard was a deadly menace and their attention was fixed on him.

When they endeavored to lend a hand to the helpless seaman he had sunk beneath the surface of the roily stream. They saw him come up and turn a ghastly face to them, but he went down like a stone before a hand could clutch at him. A few bubbles and this was the end of him. Jack Cockrell hesitated with a brave impulse to dive in search of him although he knew the bottom was a tangle of rotted trees, but just then Bill Saxby yelled to him to follow ashore with a paddle for a weapon. The luckless seaman was already drowned, this was as good as certain, and Jack jumped from the pirogue.

Blackbeard had halted his onrush and he wavered when he beheld stout Bill Saxby within a few strides of him and long Trimble Rogers galloping through the grass with his musket. Another pistol shot or two would not stop these three antagonists and a buffet from one of those hewn paddles would dash out a man's brains. The most ferocious of all pirates for once preferred to run away and live to fight another day. His boat denied him, he whirled about to plunge through the tall, matted grass. He was running in the direction of the dry knoll whence he had appeared.

Infuriated by the fate of the two seamen, Trimble Rogers made a try at shooting him on the wing but the musket ball failed to find the mark. It was necessary to hunt him down for the sake of their own safety. They might have gone their way in the pirogue but this would have been to abandon the sea-chest without an effort to drag it up or fix its location.

Now it might seem an easy matter for these pursuers, two of them young and active, to run down this fugitive Blackbeard, encumbered as he was by middle age and dissipation. They put after him boldly, with little fear of his pistols. In this dense cover he would have to fire at them haphazard and he was unlikely to tarry and wait for them. They saw him in glimpses as he fled from one grassy patch to another, or burst out of a leafy thicket, the great beard streaming over his shoulders like studding-sails, the red turban of calico a vivid blotch of color.

Nimble as they were, however, they failed to overtake him. This was because he was familiar with this landscape of bog and hummock and pine knoll. Jack Cockrell fell into a hidden quagmire and had to be fished out by main strength. Bill Saxby was caught amidst the tenacious vines, like a bull by the horns, and old Trimble came a cropper in a patch of saw-tooth palmetto. They straggled to the nearest knoll after

Blackbeard had crossed it. Then he followed a ridge which led in the direction of another of these dry islands.

The pursuers halted to gaze from this slight elevation. There was not a solitary glimpse of the crimson turban. Trimble Rogers plowed through the prickly ash, short of wind and temper, with the musket again ready for action. His language was hot enough to flash the powder in the pan.

"Lost him a'ready, ye lubbers, whilst I fetched up the rear?" he scolded. "Leave the old dog to find the trail. I be hanged if I take him alive for Stede Bonnet. What say, Bill? Skin and stuff him for a trophy———"

"First catch the slippery son o' Satan," tartly answered Bill. "He hides away like a hare. You can track him, no doubt, Trimble, but the sun will be down ere long. I'll not pass the night in this cursed puddle of a place."

Just then Jack Cockrell roved far enough to find on the knoll a small pit freshly dug, with a spade and pick beside it. Like excited children, his two comrades ran to inspect the hole which Blackbeard's seamen had dug ready for the treasure chest. Then they scattered to explore the knoll in search of signs to indicate where previous hoards might have been buried. Trimble Rogers scouted like a red Indian, eager to find traces of upturned earth, or the leaf mould disturbed, or marks of an axe on the pine trees as symbols of secret guidance. It was a futile quest, possibly because the high spring tides, when swept by easterly gales, had now and then crept back from the coast to cover the knoll and obliterate man's handiwork.

Like a hunter bewitched, the gray buccaneer was absorbed in this rare pastime until Bill Saxby exclaimed:

"Is there no wit in our addled pates? Quit this dashed folly! What of the treasure chest that was spilled from the boat?"

"It won't take wings. Wait a bit," growled Trimble. "*Madre de Dios*, but there must be more of it here. This truant Cap'n Teach knew the road well. Did ye mark how he doubled for the knoll, like a fox to its hole?"

Jack Cockrell ended the argument when he spoke up, with a shamefaced air:

"We are three heartless men! One of the seamen is drowned, rest his soul, and we could not save the poor wretch. But the other fellow was stabbed and lies in the grass near the stream. For all we know, there may be life in him."

"Heartless? 'Tis monstrous of us," cried Bill Saxby. "This greed for pirates' gold is like a poison."

They hastened to retrace their steps. The wounded seaman was breathing his last when they reached his side. They could not have prolonged his life had they remained with him. Jack Cockrell stroked his damp forehead and murmured:

"Farewell to ye, Jesse Strawn. Any message before you slip your cable?"

There was a faint whisper of:

"Scuppered, lad! Take warnin' and avast this cruel piratin' or you'll get it. A few words from the Bible 'ud ease me off."

To Jack's amazement, the veteran sinner of the lot, old Trimble Rogers, fumbled in his breeches and withdrew a small book carefully wrapped in canvas. Solemnly he hooked behind his ears a pair of huge, horn-rimmed spectacles and knelt beside the dying pirate. In the manner of a priest the buccaneer intoned a chapter of Holy Writ which he appeared to know by rote. Then he said a prayer in a powerful broken voice. Silence followed. The others waited with bared heads until Trimble said:

"His soul has passed. Shall we give the poor lad a decent burial?"

"His grave is ready. He helped dig it himself," said Bill Saxby. "And may his ghost be a torment to the fiend that slew him."

It seemed a fitting suggestion. In the freshly made treasure pit on the knoll they laid the dead pirate and used the spade to cover him. Jack Cockrell had a sheath knife with which he fashioned a rude cross and hacked on it:

JESSE STRAWN
A. D. 1718

"Aye, his ghost will flit to plague this Cap'n Teach," said Trimble Rogers. "We can leave Jesse Strawn to square his own account. Now for the sea-chest, though I misdoubt we can fish it up."

CHAPTER X

THE SEA URCHIN AND THE CARPENTER'S MATE

FOR the sake of a treasure sordid and blood-stained, it would seem shabby to overlook the fate of hapless Joe Hawkridge marooned along with the hands of the *Revenge* who were suspected of plotting mutiny.

His behavior was courageous and unselfish, for he could have fled back into the swamp when Blackbeard's wily attack threw the camp into tumult. From a sense of duty he flung himself into the fray. What friends he had in the ship were those of the decenter sort who were tired of wanton brutalities and of a master who was no better than a lunatic.

When the sloop opened fire with her guns, it was time to surrender. Unhurt save for a few scratches and a gorgeous black eye, Joe was dragged to the beach and thrown into a boat. Promptly the armed pinnace took them in tow, as arranged beforehand. Several of the prisoners had visited this rendezvous at Cherokee Inlet during a previous cruise and had some knowledge of the lay of the coast. Five or six miles out were certain shoals of sand scarcely lifted above high tide, so desolate that nothing whatever grew upon them nor was there any means of obtaining fresh water

"A pretty fancy,—to cast us where he can enjoy the sight of it when the ship sails out," said one of them who held a wounded comrade in his arms.

"Some trading vessel may sight us in the nick o' time," hopefully suggested Joe. "Never say die!"

"Trust most honest skippers to give the Inlet a wide berth," was the lugubrious reply. "This harbor was used by pirates afore Blackbeard's time. I was a silly 'prentice-boy, same as you, Joe, wi' Cap'n Willum Kidd when we lay in here to caulk his galley for the long voyage to Madagascar."

"A poor figger of a pirate was that same Kidd," spoke up another. "He ne'er scuttled a ship nor fought an action. An' his treasure was all in my eye. What did he swing for, at Execution Dock? For crackin' the skull of his gunner with a wooden bucket."

"They can't h'ist this Cap'n Teach to the same gibbet any too soon to please me, Sam," croaked a horse-faced rogue with two fingers chopped off. "He's gone and murdered all us men, as sure as blazes."

Joe Hawkridge held his peace and wondered what had become of his partner, Jack Cockrell, waiting alone in the pirogue. In the infernal commotion at the camp, Joe had failed to note whether Bill Saxby and Trimble Rogers had betaken themselves off or had been among those killed. There was the faint hope that these trusty messengers might find their way back to Captain Stede Bonnet's ship and so hasten his coming

The boats crept over the burnished surface of the harbor and passed the nearest islands which were green and wooded. Beyond them shone the gently heaving sea, with the distant gleam of a patch of sandy shoal ringed about with a necklace of surf. It was remote enough from any other land to daunt the strongest swimmer. The boats kept on until they had rounded to leeward of this ghastly prison. There was no means of resistance. The captives were driven ashore by force of arms, carrying a few of their wounded with them.

With emotions beyond the power of speech, they stared at the pinnace as the oars splashed on the return journey to the *Revenge*. Joe Hawkridge wept a little, perplexed that men could be so cruel to their own shipmates. And yet what could be expected of pirates debased enough to be Blackbeard's loyal followers? Recovering from their first stupor, the twenty able-bodied survivors began to ransack the strip of naked sand on which they had been marooned. It was no more than an acre in extent. A few small fish were found in a pool left by the falling tide and perhaps a hundred turtle eggs were uncovered during the afternoon. This merely postponed starvation.

There was not much bickering. In the shadow of certain death, these outlaws of the sea seemed to have acquired a spirit of resignation which was akin to dignity. They had lost the game. In their own lingo, it was the black spot for all hands of 'em. With the coolness of night they revived to bathe in the surf which made their thirst less hard to bear. There was not much sleep. Men walked in restless circles, looking up at the stars, muttering to themselves, or scanning the sea which had known their crimes and follies.

THEY CAPERED AND HUGGED EACH OTHER

Joe Hawkridge scooped out a bed for himself in the sand and dropped off to sleep by spells, with dreams of ease and quiet ashore and learning to be a gentleman. It was daylight when shouts startled him. The other derelicts were in a frenzy of agitation. They capered and hugged each other, and made unearthly sounds. Joe brushed the sand from his eyes and saw a small vessel approaching the tiny island. Her rig was made out to be that of a snow, which was very like a brig, the difference being in the larger main-topsail and the absence of a spanker or after steering-sail.

Such trading craft as this snow came coasting down from Salem and other New England ports to Virginia and the Carolinas laden with molasses, rum, salt, cider, mackerel, woodenware, Muscavado sugar, and dried codfish. They bartered for return cargoes and carried no specie, wherefore pirates like Stede Bonnet seldom molested them excepting to take such stores as might be needed and sometimes actually to pay for them. They were the prey of miscreants of Blackbeard's stripe who destroyed and slew for the pleasure of it.

This trim little snow was making to the southward in fancied security, having picked up a landfall, as the marooned pirates conjectured. No doubt her master had failed to receive warning that Blackbeard was in these waters and he was running his risk of encountering other marauders. He must have seen that there were people in distress on the tide-washed strip of sand. The snow shifted her helm and fired a gun. The marooned wretches could scarce credit their amazing good fortune but a grave, slow-spoken fellow who had been a carpenter's mate in the *Revenge* thought the rejoicing premature.

"When that God-fearin' skipper takes a look at us, he will sheer off and clap on sail, lads. For shipwrecked sailors you are a pizen lot o' mugs. The only blighted one of ye what's the leastwise respectable is me."

Here was a terrible misgiving which clouded the bright anticipations. They were, indeed, an unlovely cargo for the little trading vessel to take on board. One of them whipped out a pair of scissors and hastily sawed at his unkempt whiskers while his comrades stood in line and waited their turn. Others discarded gaudy kerchiefs and pistol-belts, or kicked off Spanish jack-boots. Scraps of gold lace were also unpopular. But they could not get rid of scarred faces and rum-reddened noses and the other hall-marks of their trade.

To their immense relief, the snow displayed no signs of alarm but sailed as close as the shoaling water permitted and dipped her colors. The pirates flattered themselves that they were not as frightful as the carpenter's mate had painted them. And this New England shipmaster was a merciful man who would not leave his fellow mortals to perish. They saw a boat lowered from the snow and into it jumped half a dozen sailors, soberly clad in dungaree, with round straw hats on their heads. With a gush of gratitude, the pirates swore to deal courteously by these noble merchant mariners and to repay them in whatever manner possible.

Out into the murmuring surf rushed the mild-mannered rascals, eager to grasp the boat and haul it up. It was Joe Hawkridge, hovering in the background, who raised the first cry of astonishment. His voice was so affrighted that it quavered. Before the boat was half-way from the vessel, he perceived that these were no sedate seamen from the Massachusetts Colony, even though they were in dungaree and round straw hats. He was gazing at some of Ned Rackham's evil pirates whom he had last beheld on the shattered deck of the *Plymouth Adventure* where they had been left to build a raft for themselves!

The devil had looked after his own. They had floated away from the stranded ship and instead of landing on the beach had been rescued by this unfortunate snow whose crew had been disposed of in some violent manner. This much Joe Hawkridge comprehended, although his mind was awhirl. He was better off marooned. He had helped to turn the guns of the *Plymouth Adventure* against these very same men when they had been blown out of the after cabin and the ship retaken by Captain Jonathan Wellsby.

Whatever other plans they had in store, the first business would be to kill Joe Hawkridge. This was painfully obvious. He retreated still farther behind his companions and had a confused idea of digging into the sand and burying himself from view. The discovery that these were Blackbeard's pirates in the boat created general confusion but there was no fear of instant death. It was a situation excessively awkward for the marooned company but nevertheless open to parley and argument.

By hurried agreement, the carpenter's mate, Peter Tobey by name, was chosen as spokesman. Before he began to talk with the men in the boat, Joe Hawkridge called to him in piteous accents and begged him to step back in rear of the crowd for a moment. Tobey shouted to the boat to wait outside the surf and not attempt a landing.

"What's the row, Joe?" he asked, with a kindly smile. "'Tis a disappointment for all of us,—this tangle with Rackham's crew,—but why any worse for you?"

"I can't tell it all, Peter, but my life is forfeit once they lay hands on me."

"What tarradiddle is this? As I remember it in the *Revenge*, when all hands of us were cruisin' together, ye had no mortal enemies."

"It happened in the *Plymouth Adventure*," answered Joe. "There be men in yon boat that 'ud delight in flayin' me alive. I swear it, Peter, by my mother's name. Give me up, and my blood is on your head."

The boy's words carried conviction. The stolid carpenter's mate pondered and knitted his bushy brows.

"I never did a wilful murder yet," said he. "Mallet and chisel come readier to my fist than a cutlass. Bide here, Joe. Let me get my bearings. This has the look of a ticklish matter for the lot of us. I shall be keepin' a weather eye lifted for squalls."

In mortal fear of discovery by the men in the boat, Joe flattened himself behind a palmetto log which had drifted to the other side of the island. Here he was hidden unless the boat should make a landing. The carpenter's mate waded out to join his companions who were amiably conversing with Ned Rackham's pirates. They had all been shipmates either in the *Revenge* or the *Triumph* sloop and there was boisterous curiosity concerning the divers adventures while they had been apart. Rackham's crew had been reduced to eighteen men when they were lucky enough to capture the snow, it was learned. With this small company he dared not go pirating on his own account and so had decided to rejoin Blackbeard.

"Is Ned Rackham aboard the snow?" asked Peter Tobey of the boat's coxswain.

"He is all o' that, matey, though the big bos'n of the*Plymouth Adventure* shoved a knife in his ribs to the hilt. He is flat in a bunk but he gives the orders an' it's jump at the word."

"A hard man to kill," said Peter Tobey. "Take me aboard. 'Tis best I have speech with him. Let the people wait here on the cay. They can stand another hour of it."

There was fierce protest among the marooned pirates but the carpenter's mate gruffly demanded to know if they wished to be carried into the harbor and turned over to Blackbeard. This gave the mob something to think about and they permitted the boat to pull away from them without much objection.

"A rough joke on you lads, I call it, to be dumped on this bit o' purgatory," said the coxswain to Peter Tobey. "The great Cap'n Teach must ha' been in one of his tantrums."

"It had been long brewing, as ye know," answered the carpenter's mate. "These men with you in the snow 'ud sooner follow Ned Rackham, flint-hearted though he be, than to rejoin the *Revenge*."

"Not so loud," cautioned the coxswain. "We'll see which way the cat is going to jump. Us poor devils is sore uneasy at findin' how you were dealt with."

"What of the master and crew of the snow?" asked Tobey. "Were they snuffed out? That 'ud be Rackham's way."

"No, we set 'em off in a boat, within sight of the] coast. Ned Rackham was too shrewd to bloody his hands, bein' helpless in this tub of a snow which could neither fight nor show her heels if she was chased."

Few men as there were aboard the snow, they were smartly disciplined and kept things shipshape, as Peter Tobey noted when he climbed on deck. A few minutes later he was summoned into the small cabin. Propped up in the skipper's berth, Sailing-Master Ned Rackham had a pinched and ghastly look. He was a young man, with clean-cut, handsome features, and a certain refinement of manner when he cared to assume it. The rumor was that he was the black sheep of an English house of some distinction and that he had enlisted in the Royal Navy under a false name.

"What is this mare's-nest, my good Tobey?" said he as the carpenter's mate stood diffidently fumbling with his cap. "Marooned? Twenty men of you on a reef of sand? Were ye naughty boys whilst I was absent?"

"No more than them I could name who planned to go a-cruisin' in the *Plymouth Adventure*," doggedly replied Peter Tobey who resented the tone of sneering patronage.

"Fie, fie! You talk boldly for a man in your situation. Never mind! Why the honor of this visit?"

"To make terms, Master Rackham. If us twenty men consent to serve you———"

"You babble of terms?" was the biting interruption. "I can leave you to perish on the sand, as ye no doubtdeserve, or I can carry you in with me, when I report to Captain Teach."

"But there's another choice, which hasn't escaped you," persisted the intrepid carpenter's mate. "Enlist us in your service and you'll have nigh on forty men. This snow mounts a few old swivels and you must ha' found muskets in her. With forty men, Master Rackham, there's no occasion to bow to Blackbeard's whimsies. You can h'ist the Jolly Roger for yourself and lay 'longside a bigger ship to take and cruise in. I've heard tell of a great buccaneer that started for himself in a pinnace and captured a galleon as tall as a church."

Ned Rackham's eyes flashed. Indeed, this was what he had in mind. This score of recruits would make the venture worth undertaking. Men were essential. Given enough of them to handle the snow and a boarding party besides, and he would not hesitate to shift helm and bear away to sea again.

"You will sign articles, then?" he demanded.

"Aye, I can speak for all, Master Rackham. What else is there for us? Hold fast, I would except one man. He must be granted safe conduct, on your sacred honor."

"His name, Tobey?"

"That matters not. Pledge me first. He has no more stomach for piracy and will be set ashore at some port."

"A pig in a poke?" cried Rackham, with an ugly smile. "If I refuse, what

"You will have sulky men that may turn against you some day."

"And I can leave you to rot where you are, with your nonsense of 'making terms,'" was the harsh rejoinder.

"But you won't do that," argued Peter Tobey. "Your own fortune hangs on enlisting us twenty lads. You bear Blackbeard no more love than we do."

Ned Rackham was making no great headway with this stubborn carpenter's mate who was playing strong cards of his own.

"A drawn bout, Tobey," said he, with a change of front. "No more backing and filling. You ask a small favor. Fetch your man along, whoever he may be. He shall be done no harm by me."

"Even though he made a mortal enemy of you, Master Rackham?"

"Enough, Peter. I have many enemies and scores to settle. You have my assurance but I demand the lad's name."

"Not without his permission," declared Tobey. "Set me ashore and I will confer with him."

Grudgingly Rackham consented, unwilling to have a hitch in the negotiations. In a somber humor, the carpenter's mate returned to his impatient comrades on the island. They crowded about him and he briefly delivered the message, that they were desired to cruise under Ned Rackham's flag. This delighted them, as the only way out of a fatal dilemma. Then Tobey went over tosit down upon the palmetto log behind which Joe Hawkridge still sprawled like a turtle. The anxious boy poked up his head to say:

"What cheer, Peter? A plaguey muddle you found it, I'll bet."

"Worse'n that, Joe. Rackham wouldn't clinch it with his oath unless I told him your name. I plead with him for safe conduct."

"I'd not trust his oath on a stack o' Bibles, once he set eyes on me," exclaimed Joe. "As soon put my fist to my own death warrant as go aboard with him."

"That may be," said Peter Tobey, "but you will have friends. You can't expect us to refuse to sail on account o' you."

"Leave me here, then," cried the boy. "I'll not call it deserting me. Take your men aboard the snow. Tell Ned Rackham you have the fellow amongst 'em who implored the safe conduct. Pick out some harmless lad that was saucy to Rackham in the *Revenge*, a half-wit like that Robinson younker that was the sailing-master's own cabin boy. He was allus blubberin' that Rackham 'ud kill him some day."

"No half-wit about you," admiringly quoth the carpenter's mate. "But, harkee, Joe, you will die in slow misery. Better a quick bullet from Rackham's pistol."

"Find some way to send off a little food and water, Peter, and I will set tight on this desert island. Andmayhap you will dance at the end of a rope afore I shuffle off."

"A hard request, Joe," replied the puzzled Tobey. "Unless I can come off again with some of our own men, how can it be done? Let Rackham's crew suspect I am leaving a man behind and they will rout you out."

"And they all love me, like a parson loves a pirate," grinned Joe. "I shot 'em full of spikes and bolts from a nine-pounder in the *Plymouth Adventure*."

"I shall use my best endeavor, so help me," sighed Peter Tobey. "What for did I ever quit carpenterin' to go a-piratin'? 'Tis the worst basket of chips that ever was."

"No sooner do I crawl out of one hole than I tumble into another," very truthfully observed Joe Hawkridge. "Insomuch as I've allus crawled out, you and me'll shed no more tears, Peter. There's a kick in me yet."

The disconsolate carpenter's mate returned to his fellow pirates and bade them go off to the snow. First, however, he extracted from every man the solemn promise that he would not divulge the secret of Joe Hawkridge's presence nor reveal the fact that he had remained behind. They were eager to promise anything. Several of them stole over to tell him furtive farewells. They displayed no great emotion. The trade they followed was not apt to make them turn soft over such a tragic episode as this.

When the snow was ready to take her departure, withalmost forty seasoned pirates to seek their fortunes anew, the wind died to a calm and the little vessel drifted within easy vision of the sandy island through a long afternoon. Peter Tobey tormented himself to find some pretext for smuggling food and water ashore. He invented a tale of a precious gold snuff-box which must have fallen out of his pocket and begged permission to go and search for it. But Ned Rackham sent up word that he had no notion of being delayed by a fool's errand, should a breeze spring up. He was not at all anxious to linger so close to Cherokee Inlet whence Blackbeard might sight the spars of the snow and perhaps weigh anchor in the *Revenge*.

Soon after dark the sails filled with a soft wind which drew the snow clear of the coast. Peter Tobey had been mightily busy with an empty cask. In it he stowed meat and biscuit and a bag of onions, stealthily abstracted from the storeroom while his own companions stood guard against surprise. This stuff was packed around two jugs of water tightly stoppered. Then Peter headed up the cask with professional skill and watched the opportunity to lower it from the vessel's bow where he was unseen.

The wind and tide were favorable to carrying the cask in the direction of the little patch of sea-washed sand upon which was marooned the solitary young mariner, Joe Hawkridge. The carpenter's mate saw the cask drift past the side of the snow and roll in the silverywake. Slowly it vanished in the darkness and he said to himself, in a prayer devoutly earnest:

"That boy deserves a slant o' luck, and may the good God let him have it this once. Send the cask to the beach, and I vow to go a-piratin' never again."

CHAPTER XI

JACK JOURNEYS AFOOT

IT is often said that a thing is not lost if you know where it is. This was Jack Cockrell's opinion concerning that weighty sea-chest which had splashed to the bottom of the sluggish stream in the heart of the Cherokee swamp. With young Bill Saxby and eager old Trimble Rogers he hastened from the grave of the pirate seaman whom they had buried on the knoll and fetched up at the shore where the pirogue had been left. Beside it floated Blackbeard's boat filled with water.

Having cut two or three long poles, they sounded the depth and prodded in the muddy bed to find the treasure chest. It had sunk no more than eight feet below the surface, as the tide then stood, which was not much over the head of a tall man. The end of a pole struck something solid, after considerable poking about. It was not rough, like a sunken log, and further investigation with the poles convinced them that they were thumping the lid of the chest.

"D'ye suppose you could muster breath to dive and bend a line to one o' the handles, Master Cockrell?" suggested Trimble Rogers. "Here's a coil of stout stuff in Cap'n Teach's boat what he used for a painter"The bottom of the creek is too befouled," promptly objected Jack, "and I confess it daunts me to think of meeting that drownded corpse down there. Try it yourself, if you like."

"I be needed above water to handle the musket if Blackbeard sneaks back to bang at us with his pistols," was the evasive reply. The mention of the corpse had given old Trimble a distaste for the task. To his petulant question, Bill Saxby protested that he couldn't swim a blessed stroke and he sensibly added:

"What if you did get a rope's end belayed to a handle of the chest? Even if the strain didn't part the line, we couldn't heave away in this tipsy canoe. And I am blamed certain we can't drag the chest ashore lackin' purchase and tackles."

"The smell o' treasure warps my judgment," grumpily confessed Trimble Rogers. "We ain't properly rigged to h'ist that chest from where she lays, and that's the fact."

"Give us the gear and we'd have it out and cracked open as pretty as you please," said Bill. "Set up a couple o' spars for shears, stay 'em from the bank, rig double blocks, and grapplin' irons for a diver to work with——"

"Which is exactly what Cap'n Teach will be doin' of when he finds his ship again," lamented the buccaneer.

"He will be some time findin' his ship afoot," grimlychuckled Bill. "We have naught to smash his boat with, but we'll just take it along with us."

"If we make haste to report to Captain Stede Bonnet," spoke up Jack Cockrell, "he may make sail in time to give Blackbeard other things to think on than this treasure chest. And it is my notion that the need of fitting the *Revenge* for action is too urgent to spare a crew to attempt this errand."

"We shall have it yet," cried Trimble, much consoled. "And Stede Bonnet'll blithely furnish the men and gear. For a mere babe, Master Cockrell, ye leak wisdom like a colander. Our duty is to tarry no longer at this mad business."

"The first sound word I've heard out of the old barnacle, eh, Jack?" said Bill Saxby. "We must be out of this swamp by night and layin' a course for Cap'n Bonnet and the *Royal James*."

"Whilst you empty Blackbeard's boat of water so we can tow it, let me make a rude chart," was Jack's happy idea. "Some mishap or other may overtake us ere we get the chance to seek the treasure again. And our own memory of this pest-hole of a swamp may trick us."

Bill Saxby's tattered diary supplied a scrap of paper and Jack dug charred splinters from the inside of the canoe which enabled him to draw a charcoal sketch or map. It traced the smaller stream from the fork where it had branched off, the stretch in which it widened like a tiny lagoon or bayou, and the point of shore just beyond which the pirogue had unexpectedly rammed Blackbeard's boat. A cross designated the spot where the treasure chest had sunk in eight feet of water.

The knoll and the grave of Seaman Jesse Strawn were also indicated, with the distance estimated in paces and the bearings set down by the position of the sun.

"There," said Jack, well pleased with his handiwork, "and once we are aboard ship, I can make fair copies on parchment, one for each of us."

"Thankee, lad," gratefully exclaimed Trimble Rogers who now had something to live for. "'Twas a fond dream o' mine, when I sailed wi' the great Cap'n Edward Davis in the South Sea, some day to blink at a chart what showed where the gold was hid."

They were, indeed, recovered from the intoxication of treasure and recalled to realizing the obligation that was upon them. They had swerved from it but now they pressed forward to finish the appointed journey. The canoe moved down to the fork of the waters with the light cock-boat skittering in its wake and perhaps the unhappy Blackbeard, stranded in the swamp, hurled after them a volley of those curses for which he was renowned. Once Jack Cockrell laughed aloud, explaining to his laboring comrades:

"Captain Teach will be combing the burrs from his grand beard when he boards his ship again. He may get hung by the chin in a thicket

"He's sure to spend this night in the swamp, blast him," earnestly observed Bill, "and the mosquitoes'll riddle his hide."

"And may Jesse Strawn lose no time in hauntin' him," said Trimble Rogers.

There was an hour of daylight to spare when they had ascended the larger creek as far as the canoe could be paddled. There they disembarked and hid the dugout and the cock-boat in the overhanging bushes where they could be found again in case of a forced retreat. Bill and Jack burdened themselves with the sack of food and the water jug while the old buccaneer set out in the lead as a guide. It was irksome progress for a time, but gradually the ground became drier and the foliage was more open. Dusk found them safely emerged from the great Cherokee swamp and in a pleasant forest of long-leaf pine with a carpet of brown needles.

In fear of Indians, they dared not kindle a fire and so stretched themselves in their wet and muddy rags and slept like dead men. What awakened Jack Cockrell before sunrise was a series of groans from Trimble Rogers who sat with his back against a tree while he rubbed his legs. Ashamed at being heard, he grumpily explained:

"Cord and faggot 'ud torment me no worse than this hell-begotten rheumatism. I be free of it in a ship but the land reeks with foul vapors. It hurt me cruel at Cartagena in the year of

"But can you walk all day, in such misery as that?" anxiously interrupted Jack.

"If not, I'll make shift to crawl," said the old sea dog.

It was apparent to Jack and also to Bill Saxby that the ordeal of the swamp had crippled their companion whose bodily strength had been overtaxed. They debated whether to try to return to the coast and risk a voyage in the canoe but Trimble Rogers swore by all the saints in the calendar that he was done with the pestilent swamp. He would push on in spite of the rheumatism. His hardy spirit was unbroken. And so they resumed the march, the suffering buccaneer hobbling with the musket as a staff or with a strong arm supporting him.

Halts were frequent and progress very slow. Now and then they had glimpses of the blue sea and so knew that they held the course true. It had been reckoned that two days would suffice to bring them to the bay in which Stede Bonnet's ship was anchored. By noon of this first day, however, it was plainly evident that Trimble Rogers was done for. He uttered no complaints, and withheld the groans behind his set teeth, but his lank body was a-tremble with pain and fatigue. Whenever he sank down to rest they had to raise him up and set him on his legs again before he could totter a little way farther.

"What say, Jack, to slingin' him on a pole, neck andheels?" suggested Bill Saxby. "Can we make him fast with our belts?"

"And choke him to death? In Charles Town I saw Captain Bonnet's pirates carry their wounded in litters woven of boughs."

The suffering Trimble put a stop to this by shouting:

"Avast wi' the maunderin' nonsense! Push on, lads, and leave this old hulk be. Many a goodly man have I seen drop in the jungle. What matters it? Speed ye to Cap'n Bonnet."

"Here is one pirate that won't desert a shipmate," declared Bill Saxby. "And how can we push on without you, old True-Penny, to lay your nose to the trail? I took no heed o' the marks and landfalls."

"Like a sailor ashore, mouth open and eyes shut," rasped the buccaneer of Hispaniola.

"Methinks I might find my way in this Carolina country," ventured Jack Cockrell. "It would be easier for a landsman like myself than for Bill who is city-bred and a seaman besides."

"More wisdom from the stripling," said Trimble. "Willing as I be to die sooner than delay ye and so vex Stede Bonnet, it 'ud please me to live to overhaul that sea chest of Blackbeard's."

"I'll stand by this condemned old relic," amiably agreed Bill Saxby. "Do you request Cap'n Bonnet to send a party to salvage us, Jack."

"He will take pleasure in it, Bill. Before I go letme help you find shelter,—dry limbs for props and a thatch of palmetto leaves."

"Take no thought of us," urged Trimble. "Trust me to set this lazy oaf to work. Now listen, Jack, and carefully. Cap'n Bonnet's ship waits in the Cape Fear River, twelve leagues to the north'ard of us. You will find her betwixt a bay of the mainland and a big-sized island where the river makes in from the sea. There will be a lookout kept and I can tell ye where to meet a boat."

With a memory as retentive as a printed page, the keen-eyed old wanderer described the landscape league by league, the streams and their direction, the hills which were prominent, the broad stretches of savannah or grassy meadow, the belts of pine forest, the tongues of swamp which had to be avoided. Jack was compelled to repeat the detailed instructions over and over, and he was a far more studious pupil than when snuffy Parson Throckmorton had rapped his knuckles and fired him with rebellious dreams of piracy. At length, the buccaneer was willing to acknowledge:

"Unless an Indian drive an arrow through the lad's brisket, Bill, I can trust him to find our ship. Best give him the musket."

"Me shoulder that carronade and trudge a dozen leagues?" objected Jack. "I travel light and leave the ordnance with you."

They insisted on his taking more than a third of thefood but he refused to deprive them of the water jug. There would be streams enough to slake his thirst. It was an affectionate parting. Bill Saxby's innocent blue eyes were suffused and his chubby face sorrowful at the thought that they might not meet again. Trimble Rogers fished out his battered little Bible and quoted a few verses, as appeared to be his habit on all solemn occasions. Jack Cockrell knew him well enough by now to find it not incongruous. Among this vanishing race of sea fighters had been many a hero of the most fervent piety. Their spirit was akin to that of Francis Drake who summoned his crew to prayers before he cleared for action.

And in this wise did Master Jack Cockrell set out to bear a message from comrades in dire distress. Moreover, in his hands were the lives of Joe Hawkridge and those other marooned seamen, as he had every reason to believe. It was a grave responsibility to be thrust upon a raw lad in his teens who had been so carefully nurtured by his fretful guardian of an uncle, Mr. Peter Arbuthnot Forbes. Jack thought of this and said to himself, with a smile:

"A few weeks gone, and I was locked in my room without any dinner for loitering with Stede Bonnet's pirates at the Charles Town tavern. My education has been swift since then."

He was expectant of meeting no end of peril and hardship and he fought down a sense of dread that wasnot to his discredit. But it was so decreed that he should pass secure and unmolested. At first he went too fast, without husbanding his strength, and loped along like a hound whenever the country was clear of brushwood. This wore him down and he failed to watch carefully enough for his landmarks. Toward the end of the day he became confused because he could not discern the sea even by climbing a tree. But he tried to keep bearing to the northeast until the sun went down. Afraid of losing himself entirely and ignorant of the lay of the land by night, he made his bivouac in a grove of sycamore saplings and imagined Indians were creeping up whenever the leaves rustled.

This fear of roaming savages troubled him next day as he wearily trudged through this primeval wilderness unknown to white settlers. It spurred him on despite his foot-sore fatigue and he was making the journey more rapidly than old Trimble Rogers, for all his cunning woodcraft, had been able to accomplish it. Almost at the end of his endurance, the plucky lad discerned the sheen of a broad water in the twilight and so came to the Cape Fear River.

He had worried greatly lest he might have veered too far inland but there was the wooded bay and the fore-land crowned with dead pines which had been swept by forest fire. And out beyond it was the island, of the size and shape described by Trimble Rogers, making a harbor from the sea which rolled to the horizon rim

But no tall brig, nor any other vessel rode at anchor in this silent and lonely haven. Jack had been told precisely where to look for it. He had made no mistake. Some emergency had caused Captain Stede Bonnet to make sail and away.

A king's ship or some other hostile force might have compelled him to slip his cable in haste, reflected Jack as he descended to the shore of the bay. It was most unlike the chivalrous Stede Bonnet to abandon two of his faithful seamen without an effort to succor them. Endeavoring to comfort himself with this surmise, the sorely disappointed boy paced the sand far into the night and gazed in vain for the glimmer of a fire or the spark of a signal lantern in a ship's rigging. He could not bear to think of the dark prospect should no help betide him.

Some time before day he was between waking and sleeping when a queer delusion distracted him. Humming in his ears was the refrain of a song which was both familiar and hauntingly pleasant. It seemed to charm away his poignant anxieties, to lull him with a feeling of safety. He wondered if his troublesome adventures had made him light-headed. He moved not a muscle but listened to this phantom music and noted that it sounded louder and clearer instead of fading away.

And still he refused to believe that it was anything more than a drowsy mockery.

At length a vagrant breeze brought him a snatch of this enjoyable chorus in deeper, stronger volume and he leaped to his feet with a shout. It was no hallucination. Lusty seamen were singing in time to the beat of their oars, and Jack Cockrell knew it for the favorite song of Stede Bonnet's crew. He could distinguish the words as they rolled them out in buoyant, stentorian harmony:

"An' when my precious leg was lopt,
Just for a bit of fun
I picks it up, on t'other hopt,
An' rammed it in a gun.
'What's that for?' cries out Ginger Dick,
'What for? my jumpin' beau?
Why, to give the lubbers one more kick,'
Yo, ho, with the rum below!"

CHAPTER XII

A PRIVATE ACCOUNT TO SETTLE

THE ship's boat was bound into the bay, probably to lie there for daybreak, and Jack Cockrell rushed down to the beach where he set up such a frantic hullabaloo that the sailors ceased singing and held their breath and their oars suspended. They had come to look for Bill Saxby and Trimble Rogers, but this was a strange voice. It was so odd a circumstance that several of them hailed the shore with questions loud and perplexed.

"Master John Cockrell, at your service," came back the reply. "Captain Bonnet knows me. I am the lad that clouted a six-foot pirate of yours for being saucy to a maid in Charles Town."

This aroused a roar of laughter and there were gusty shouts of:

"Here's that same Will Brant in the boat with us. He shakes in his boots at the sound of ye."

"What's the game, lad? Have ye taken a ship of your own to scour the Main?"

Jack ignored this good-natured badinage and, in dignified accents, told them to come ashore and take him off to the *Royal James*. In this company he had a reputation to live up to as a man of parts and valor. They let the boat ground on the smooth sand and one of them lighted a torch of pitch-pine splinters. The fine young gentleman who had strolled arm-in-arm with Stede Bonnet to the tavern green was a ragged scarecrow and bedaubed with red clay and black mud. This aroused their sympathy before he told them of his escape from the *Revenge* and his adventures with Bill Saxby and the crippled buccaneer. In their turn they explained how Captain Bonnet had sent them down the river to await the return of the two men who were now stranded in the wilderness two days' march distant.

"And why did your captain shift the brig from her anchorage off the island?" asked Jack.

This amused the boat's crew who nudged each other and were evasive until the master's mate who was in charge went far enough to say:

"A sloop came in from the Pamlico River. Our ship sought a snugger harbor, d'ye see? There was some private business. We loaded the sloop with hogshead of sugar, and bolts of damask, and silver ingots. His Excellency, Governor Eden, of the North Carolina Province, turns an honest penny now and then."

"The Governor of this Province is a partner in piracy?" cried Jack.

"Brawl it not so loud, nor spill it to Cap'n Bonnetcautioned the master's mate. "I confide this much to stave off your foolish questions when ye board the ship."

There was no reason to tarry in the bay and the boat pulled out to follow the course of the river and return in haste to the brig *Royal James* in her more secluded harbor. The news that Blackbeard was at his old rendezvous within easy sail to the southward eclipsed all other topics. And when it was learned that he had lost the two sloops of his squadron, there was fierce delight. Although the *Revenge* was a larger vessel and more heavily manned and gunned, they were hilariously confident of victory. It was a burning grudge and a private quarrel, and fuel was added to the flame by the tidings that a score or more of seamen had been mercilessly marooned to perish because of their suspected preference for Captain Stede Bonnet.

When Jack Cockrell caught sight of the shapely brig as she loomed in the morning haze, it seemed as though years had passed since he had enviously watched her pass out over the Charles Town bar. Presently he spied the soldierly captain on the quarter-deck, his spare figure all taut and erect, his chin clean-shaven, his queue powdered, his apparel fresh and in good taste. A ship is like her master and the watch was sluicing down decks or setting up the rigging which had slackened with the heavy dew. Jack felt ashamed to let himself be seen. This was no place for a ragamuffin.

Captain Bonnet strode to the gangway and stareddown at this bit of human flotsam. He was quick to recognize his boyish friend and admirer and ordered the men to lower a boatswain's chair and lift Master Cockrell aboard. Jack was, indeed, so stiffened and sore and weary that he had been wondering how he could climb the side of a ship.

"Tut, tut, my son, bide your time," exclaimed Stede Bonnet as they met on deck. "Tell it later. The master's mate will enlighten me."

He led the way into the cabin which was in order and simply furnished. One servant brewed fragrant coffee from Arabia while another made a room ready for the guest and fetched clean clothing from the captain's chests and a tub of hot water. And as soon as the grateful Master Cockrell had made himself presentable, he was invited to sit down at table with the captain and enjoy a meal of porridge and crisp English bacon and fresh eggs from the ship's hen-coop in the long-boat and hot crumpets and marmalade. And this after the pinched ration of mouldy salt-horse and wormy hard-bread! Captain Bonnet lighted a roll of tobacco leaves, which he called a *cigarro*, and puffed clouds of smoke while Master Cockrell cleaned every dish and lamented that his skin felt too tight to begin all over again.

He was now in a mood to relate his strange yarn, from its outset in the ill-fated merchant trader, *Plymouth Adventure*. Eagerly he begged information concerning her people after their shipwreck, but Captain Bonnet had been cruising far offshore to intercept a convoy of rich West Indiamen from Jamaica for the old country.

"I will make it my duty to set you ashore at Charles Town, Master Jack," said he, "and I pray you may find your good uncle alive and still vowing to hang all rogues of pirates."

"But I must sail with you, sir, till you have saved Joe Hawkridge and his shipmates and blown Blackbeard out of water."

"Rest easy on that," exclaimed Stede Bonnet. "Those affairs are most urgent. My ship will drop down the river to-day, with the turn o' the tide, and heave to long enough to land a party, six men, to go in search of Trimble Rogers who is the apple of my eye. I shall not ask you to join them, but you can give directions and pen a fair map, I trow."

"Gladly would I go," replied Jack, "but my poor legs wobble like your valiant old buccaneer's. And my feet are raw."

"You have proved yourself," was the fine compliment. "I judged ye aright when we first met."

Soon the deck above them resounded to the tramp of boots and the thump of sheet-blocks as the brisk seamen made ready to cast the ship free. She was in competent hands and so Stede Bonnet lingered below to enjoy talking with the youth whose manners and breeding were like his own. In a mood unusually confidential he confirmed Jack's earlier impressions, that he was a pirate with a certain code of honor which reminded one of Robin Hood of Sherwood Forest who robbed the rich and befriended the poor. Touching on his mortal quarrel with Blackbeard, he revealed how that traitorous ruffian had proposed a partnership while he, Stede Bonnet, was a novice at the trade. The plot all hatched to take Bonnet's fine ship, the *Revenge*, from him, Blackbeard had disclosed his hand at the final conference when he said, with a sarcastic grimace:

"I see, my good sir, that you are not used to the cares and duties of commanding a vessel, so I will relieve you of 'em."

As soon as Captain Bonnet had mended his fortunes and had the goodly brig *Royal James* to cruise in, his ruling purpose was to regain the *Revenge* from Blackbeard and at the same time wreak a proper punishment.

"So now if we can trap this black-hearted Teach before he flits to sea," said Stede Bonnet, "you will see a pretty engagement, Master Cockrell. But first we must find the score o' men that he marooned. It will be a deed of mercy, besides affording me a stronger crew."

The brig was soon standing down the river while the landing party broke out an ample store of provisions and powder and ball, with canvas for a tent. The plan was for them to pitch a camp near the shore of the bay to which they could fetch back Trimble Rogers and Bill Saxby and there wait for their ship to return and take them off. They were ready to go ashore when CaptainBonnet's navigator ordered the main-topsail laid aback and the brig slowly swung into the wind. The delay was brief and no sooner was the boat cast off than the *Royal James* proceeded on the voyage to Cherokee Inlet.

Clumsy as those sailing ships of two hundred years ago appear to modern eyes, their lines were finely moulded under water and with a favoring wind they could log a fair distance in a day's run. It goes without saying that this tall brig was shoved along for all she was worth before a humming breeze that made her creak, and during the night she was reckoned to be a few miles to seaward of the sandy islands which extended like a barrier outside of Cherokee Inlet. Jack Cockrell stood a watch of his own, dead weary but with no thought of sleep until he could hear the lookout shout "Land ho!"

This cry came from aloft soon after dawn. The brig moved toward the nearest of these exposed shoals while her officers consulted a chart spread upon the cabin roof. They were wary of running the ship aground with Blackbeard no more than a few miles distant. So bare were these yellow patches of sand that showed against the green water that a group of men on any one of them would have been easily discernible. The *Royal James* coasted along outside of them under shortened sail but discovered nothing to indicate a party of marooned seamen

"But they must be out here somewhere," cried Jack Cockrell, in great distress.

"They ought to be, for no trading vessel would take 'em off," replied the puzzled Captain Bonnet. "And if they were towed out in boats as ye say, Jack, these islands must ha' been where they were beached."

"But you won't give up the search, sir, without another tack past those outermost shoals?"

"Oh, we shall rake them all, but Blackbeard may have changed that crotchety mind of his and taken the men back to his ship."

"I fear I have seen the last of my dear Joe Hawkridge," exclaimed Jack.

"From what you tell me, the young scamp is not so easily disposed of," smiled Captain Bonnet. "I must haul out to sea ere long. 'Tis poor business to let Blackbeard glimpse my spars and so take warning."

This was sad news and Jack walked away to hide his quivering lip. To examine the islands again was a forlorn hope because already it seemed certain that nothing alive moved on any of them. The brig passed them closer than before as she made a long reach before turning out to sea. It was the intention to sail in to engage Blackbeard very early the next morning and meanwhile he would be vigilantly blockaded.

Even Jack Cockrell, hopeful to the last, was compelled to agree with the crew of the brig that not a solitary man could be seen on these sea-girt cays and it seemed useless to send off a boat to explore them one by one. There would have been some stir or signal, even if men were too weak to stand. The air was clear and from the brig's masts it was possible to sweep every foot of sandy surface. Here was another mystery of the sea. It occurred to Stede Bonnet to ask:

"You took it for granted they were marooned, Jack, when the boats passed from your sight and you were hidden in the tree in the swamp. What if a quicker death were dealt 'em?"

"That may be, sir."

The brig was leaving the coast astern. Jack moped by himself until his curiosity was drawn to a group of seamen upon the forecastle head who were talking loudly and pointing at something in the water, well ahead of the ship. One vowed it was a big sea-turtle asleep, another was willing to wager his silver-mounted pistols that it was a rum barrel, while a third announced that he'd stake his head on its being a mermaid or her husband. The after-deck brought a spy-glass to bear and perceived that the thing was splashing about. The tiller was shifted to bring it close aboard and soon Captain Bonnet exclaimed that it was, indeed, a merman a-cruising with a cask!

Jack Cockrell scampered to the heel of the bowsprit to investigate this ocean prodigy. And as the cask drifted nearer he saw that Joe Hawkridge was clingingto it. There was no mistaking that dauntless grin and the mop of carroty hair. A handy seaman tossed a bight of line over his shoulders as he bobbed past the forefoot of the brig and he was yanked bodily over the bulwark like a strange species of fish. Flopping on deck he waved a skinny arm in greeting and then Jack Cockrell rushed at him, lifted him bodily, and dragged him to the cabin.

"What ho, comrade!" said the dripping merman. "Blast my eyes, but I was sick with worry for you. I left you in that swamp——"

"And I thought you dead, Joe. For the love o' heaven, tell me how you fared and what——"

Captain Bonnet interfered to say:

"I treated you more courteously than this, Jack. Let us make him comfortable."

Accepting the rebuke, Jack bustled his amazing friend into a change of clothes and saw that he was well fed. Little the worse for his watery pilgrimage, Joe Hawkridge explained at his leisure:

"Ned Rackham took the others away in the snow, as I tell ye, Cap'n Bonnet, and there was I in the doleful dumps. Prayers get answered and miracles do happen, for next day there come a-floatin' to the beach a cask full of grub and water. Good Peter Tobey, the carpenter's mate, had a hand in launchin' it, no doubt, but the Lord hisself steered the blessed cask. Well, while I set a-giving thanks and thinkin' one thing an' another, I figgered that when I'd ate all the grub and swigged the water, I was no further along."

"And so you thought you would trust the Lord again," suggested Captain Bonnet.

"Aye, sir, that was it. By watchin' the tides I reckoned I might drift to another island and so work to the coast, taking my provisions with me. There was some small line in the cask that Peter Tobey had wrapped the stores in, and I knotted a harness about the cask that I could slip an arm in, and off I goes when the tide sets right. But some kind of a dratted cross-current ketched me and I'm sailin' out to sea, I finds, without compass or cross-staff. Bound to get to London River, eh, Jack, same as we started out on the silly little raft."

"Whew, this adventure was bad enough," cried Jack, "but when you saw Ned Rackham's pirates in the boat, and you couldn't run away,—I wonder, honest, Joe, you didn't die of fright."

"What for? This is no trade for a nervous wight. And now for a bloody frolic with Blackbeard's bullies."

"There is a share of his treasure for you, Joe, as soon as we can go find it," gleefully announced Master Cockrell. "I have the chart drawn all true with mine own hand. Let me get it."

While the two lads pored entranced over the map of the branching creek and the pine-covered knoll, the crew of the *Royal James* were overhauling weapons and clearing the ship for action. It disappointed them tolack the twenty men whom they had expected to find marooned but this made them no less eager for battle. Concerning Ned Rackham, there was no feud with him or grudge to square and he could go his way in the little trading snow without fear of molestation from Stede Bonnet.

Under cover of night the *Royal James* worked back to the sandy islands and anchored in the channel. One of her boats had ventured within sight of the Inlet for a stealthy reconnaissance and reported that the *Revenge* was still in the harbor. Captain Bonnet was considering his plan of attack. He said nothing about it to Jack Cockrell and his chum, the merman, and they greedily listened to the gossip of the petty officers or thrashed out theories of their own.

To sail boldly into the harbor was a ticklish risk to run as there was no pilot aboard who knew the inner channel and the depths of water. All the gunners were in favor of attempting it because they yearned to settle it with crashing broadsides. But the battered, hairy sea-dogs who had fought it out in hand-to-hand conflicts on the Caribbean were for leaving the brig in safe water and sending fifty men in boats to board the *Revenge* at the first break of day.

In the midst of the fo'castle argument, Captain Bonnet sent for Jack Cockrell and told him:

"You are to keep out of harm's way, my young gamecock. I have undertaken to deliver you to your esteemed uncle with arms and legs intact, and your head on your shoulders."

"But I am lusty enough to poke about with a pike or serve at a gun tackle," protested the unhappy Master Cockrell.

"I expect you to obey me," was the stern mandate. "You will have company. This Joe Hawkridge is to stay with you."

"But he is a rare hand in a fight, Captain Bonnet. You should have seen him in the *Plymouth Adventure*."

"The boy is weak and all unstrung, though he carries it bravely, Jack. And Blackbeard's men would take special pains to kill him as a deserter."

By this humane verdict the two lads were shielded from peril, as far as it lay within Stede Bonnet's power. They should have felt grateful to him but on the contrary it made them quite peevish and they sulked by themselves up in the bow of the ship until it was time to eat again. Then their gnawing appetites persuaded them to forgive their considerate host.

The pirates moved about the deck until far into the night while the sparks flew from cutlass blades pressed to the whirling grindstone. Tubs were filled with hand-grenades and fire-pots, the deck strewn with sand, the magazine opened and powder passed up. Stede Bonnet was careful to see for himself that all things were in order. At such times he was a martinet of a soldier.

Anxiously he watched the weather signs, as did everyseasoned sailor on board. It bade fair to be a bright morning with an easterly air and this would carry the brig into the harbor with the minimum danger of stranding if the lead were cast often enough. Joe Hawkridge and Jack Cockrell were of some assistance in explaining the marks and bearings of the channel, and Captain Bonnet consulted them over the chart unrolled upon the cabin table. He had made up his mind to sail the brig in and risk the hazards of shoal water. When he went on deck, Jack thought of a topic as thrilling as this imminent duel between ships and he remarked with joyous excitement:

"Now, Joe, as soon as ever Blackbeard gets his drubbing, we beg a boat and men and gear of Captain Bonnet and go up the creek to fish out the treasure chest and dig in the knoll."

"Hook your fish before you fry 'em," replied the sagacious apprentice-boy. "This scrummage with the *Revenge* will be no dancin' heel-and-toe. A bigger ship, more guns and men, and a Blackbeard who will fight like a demon when he's cornered. Crazy though he may be, he is the most dangerous pirate afloat."

CHAPTER XIII

OUR HEROES SEEK SECLUSION

AN hour before dawn the anchor was aweigh and the *Royal James* drifted ahead like a shadow, in between the outer islands where the fairway was wide and safe. Her gun-ports were open and every man was alertly at his station. It was a silent ship excepting when an officer passed an order along. Joe Hawkridge began to feel more sanguine of winning against odds. He had never seen such iron discipline as this in the bedlam aboard the *Revenge*. Stede Bonnet knew how to slacken the reins and when to apply the curb. His men were loyal because he dealt out justice as well as severity.

"The captain says we must go below when the action commences, Joe," dismally observed Jack Cockrell.

"It goes against the grain but we will not dispute him," was the sage reply. "We needn't be idle. You can lend a hand with the powder or pass the water buckets to douse the fire if she gets ablaze. And there's the wounded to carry into the cockpit and the blood to mop up, and——"

"Enough o' that," cried Jack, getting pale about the gills. "You take it like a butcher!"

"What else is it, you big moon-calf? Set me safe ashore in that Charles Town of yours, and I hope ne'er to see another weapon barring a spoon and a knife to cut my vittles."

"There is sense in that," agreed young Master Cockrell.

Smartly handled, the brig crept in as far as she dared go without more light by which to avoid the shallower water. The anchor was dropped to a short cable and buoyed ready to slip. It was estimated that the distance from Blackbeard's ship was somewhat more than a mile. The stars faded and the cloudless sky began to take on a roseate hue. The light breeze which had breathed like a cool zephyr through the night was dying in languid catspaws. Gradually the dark outline of coastal swamp and forest was uncurtained. And eager eyes were able to discern the yellow spars and blurred hull of the *Revenge* against the gloomy background.

Stede Bonnet's brig was, of course, pricked out much more sharply with the seaward horizon behind her. To her crew, in this hushed morning, there came a prolonged, shrill note that was like the call of a bird. It trilled with a silvery sweetness and was repeated over and over again.

"A bos'n's pipe," said Captain Bonnet, a hand cupped at his ear. "Blackbeard has sighted us and is mustering his crew."

So faint was the breeze that the command was given to man two boats and take a hawser from the brig to tow her through the inner channel. Before they were in motion, however, the pearly mist began to roll out of the Cherokee swamp as if a great cauldron were steaming. The weather favored it, heat in the air and little wind. The mist seemed also to rise from the water, hanging low but as thick as a summer fog. It shrouded the coast and Blackbeard's ship and crept out across the harbor until the brig was enveloped in it.

"'Twas like this when we swum ashore and found the pirogue, Cap'n Bonnet," said Joe Hawkridge. "A curious kind o' white smother from the swamp."

"And how long did it hang thus?" was the impatient query.

"When the sun was well up, sir, it seemed to burn away like. It has the same look as the fever-breedin' vapors of Darien and Yucatan."

Captain Bonnet called his boats back and was in an ugly humor. There was no towing the brig through this bothersome fog which obscured every mark and left a man bewildered. And instead of surprising Blackbeard unprepared, he would now have time to make his ship ready. However, Stede Bonnet was not a man to wring his hands because a well-laid scheme went wrong. Without delay the crew was assembled in the waist and he spoke to them from the break of the poop.

"We shall make this weather serve our purpose, lads. Fill the boats, every man to his billet. The mates willsee to it that the oars are well muffled. Silence above all things. Nimbly now."

There was no need to say more. They fathomed the strategy which would enable them to approach Blackbeard's ship unheard and unseen and then swarm over her side in a ferocious onslaught. Cheerily they took stock of their weapons, drank a health from a tub of stiff grog, and lined up for Captain Bonnet's inspection. They wore clean clothes, the best they could find in their bags, as has always been the sailor's habit when going into action. The ship was left in charge of the navigator with a few men who were the least stalwart or experienced in such desperate adventures as this.

Stede Bonnet went in command of the largest boat to lead the party and single out Blackbeard as his own particular foe. There was a large chance that he might not return and he therefore left instructions for the disposal of the brig, advising the navigator to take her to Charles Town and there sue for the king's pardon in behalf of those on board. He shook hands with Jack Cockrell and Joe Hawkridge, bade them be careful of their own safety, and with no more ado took his place in the boat. The flotilla stole away from the brig, sunburned, savage men with bright weapons for whom life was like a throw of the dice, and the pearly fog concealed them when they had passed no more than a cable-length away. So skilfully was the sound of the oars deadened that you wouldnot have guessed that boats were moving across the harbor.

"Blackbeard fights like a tiger but trust Cap'n Bonnet to outwit him," said Joe Hawkridge, who stood at the brig's rail with Jack at his elbow.

"It will be mighty hard waiting," was the tense reply. "We shall know when they find the *Revenge*. They are not apt to miss her, with a compass in the captain's boat."

"Aye, there'll be noise enough. Plaguey queer, eh, Jack, to be a-loafin' with nothing to see, like your head was wrapped in a blanket. They ought to fetch alongside Blackbeard in a half-hour. Go turn the sand-glass in the cabin."

They fidgeted about in aimless fashion and fell into talk with the navigator, or artist, as he was called, a middle-aged man who had been a master mariner in the slave trade. He told them a yarn or two of the Guinea coast but he, too, was restless and left them to stump up and down the deck and peer toward the shore. Jack dodged into the cabin to watch the sand trickle into the bottom of the glass. Never was a half-hour so long in passing.

A yell from Joe Hawkridge recalled him to the deck. He listened but heard no distant pistol shots or the hoarse uproar of men in mortal combat. Joe raised a warning hand and told him to stand still. There came a faint splash. It might have been a fish leaping but Joe insisted that it was made by a careless oar. Jack heard it again and then fancied he caught the softened beat of muffled oars close at hand.

"They lost the course. The fog confused 'em," said he, in great disgust.

"But why come back to the ship?" demanded Joe. "They could lay and wait for the fog to lift a little. And I told Cap'n Bonnet to bear to the north'ard if in doubt and find the shore of the swamp. Then he could coast back to the beach and so strike the *Revenge*."

"Well, here they come, Joe, and there is sure to be a good reason. Mayhap the fog cleared to landward and they intend to tow the brig in, after all."

Just then the foremost boat became visible and behind it was the vague shape of another. The puzzled lads stared and stared and the hair stiffened on their scalps for sheer horror. These were not the boats from the *Royal James*. They were filled with Blackbeard's own pirates from the *Revenge*!

The explanation was simple enough. Joe Hawkridge read it at a glance. Blackbeard was not the drunken chuckle-head that Stede Bonnet had assumed him to be. He, too, had taken advantage of the fog to attempt to carry the enemy by stealth. The wit of the one had been matched by the other. And the two flotillas had gone wide enough in passing to escape mutual discovery. In a way it was a pirates' comedy but there were two spectators who foresaw a personal tragedyThey fled for the cabin and scuttled through a small door in a bulkhead which admitted them to the dark hold of the ship.

It was their purpose to hide in the remotest nook that could be found. Falling over odds and ends of cargo they burrowed like rats and stowed themselves behind a tier of mahogany logs which had been taken out of some prize or other. They were in the bottom of the ship, upon the rough floor covering the stone ballast. Then these frightened stowaways found respite to confer in tremulous whispers.

"This is the very dreadfulest fix of all, Joe. I had a fair look at Blackbeard himself, in the stern of the boat,—red ribbons in his whiskers, and his sash stuck full of pistols."

"That old rip isn't an easy man to mistake, Jack. Now the fat *is* in the fire," replied the Hawkridge lad who, for once, appeared discouraged. "Cap'n Bonnet is a vast sight happier than us. He gets the *Revenge* without strikin' a blow."

"But Blackbeard gets *us*," wailed Master Cockrell. "And I helped to chase him through the swamp after we rammed the pirogue into his wherry and capsized the treasure chest. Do you suppose he knew me just now?"

"Those little red eyes of his are passing keen. But didn't ye tell me of smearing your face with mud that day to fend off the mosquitoes? It may ha' disguised you." "A little comfort in that, Joe, but to be found in Stede Bonnet's brig bodes ill enough. Of a truth we be born to trouble as the sparks fly upward ever since we joined the pirates. What is your advice?"

"To stay hid below and pray God for another shift o' fortune," piously answered Joe. "There is no fear of Blackbeard's rummagin' the hold at present. He must decide if he'll fight the *Revenge* or give her the slip. And whilst him and his men are busied on deck, I can make bold to search for stores fit to eat. Cap'n Bonnet allus had a well-found ship. Blast it, Jack, my hearty, stock us up and we could lie tucked in the forepeak for a month o' Sundays."

"But the rats and the darkness and the stinks, and to be expecting discovery," was Jack's dreary comment.

"It would ha' looked like a parlor to me when I was on that barren cay and sighted Ned Rackham's rogues coming off from the snow," said the other stowaway. He was beginning to recuperate from the shock.

They were in a mood for no more speech but sat in this rayless cavern of a hold and strove to hear any sounds which might indicate the course of events on deck. There was no hubbub of firearms nor the cries of wounded men. It was foolish to assume that the dozen seamen who had been left to keep the ship would attempt resisting Blackbeard's mob of pirates all primed for slaughter. When quietude seemed to reign all through the ship Joe Hawkridge whispered this opinion

"If his fancy was to deal with 'em later, he would pitch the lot down here in the hold. Failing that, Jack, he has offered 'em the chance to enlist. Being so few, they can't plot mischief, and he has lost the hands he left aboard the *Revenge*."

"But I thought all this crew was true as steel to Stede Bonnet, Joe."

"Many a man'll change his mind to save his life," was the reply. "And these lads aren't what you call Cap'n Bonnet's picked men. As for the navigator, Blackbeard needs him to fill Ned Rackham's berth."

Soon Joe Hawkridge told Jack to stay where he was. Now was the time to explore the lower part of the ship. Squeezing his comrade's hand in farewell, Joe crawled aft to make his way to a rough bulkhead which walled off a storeroom built next to the cabin. The boys had passed through it in their headlong flight below. Here was kept the bulk of the ship's provisions. Joe Hawkridge had learned of the storeroom through helping the steward hoist out a barrel of pork.

With his heart in his throat the venturesome lad groped like a blind man, grievously barking his shins and his knuckles, until he bumped into the timbers of the bulkhead. Inching himself along, he came to the small door which had been cut into the hold to connect with the main hatch. He had slipped the iron bar behind him during his flight with Jack Cockrell. Pulling the door ajar he wormed through into the storeroom whichwas also dark as midnight. His fingers touched what seemed to be a tierce of beef but he had no tools to start the head or the hoops. In the same manner he discovered other casks and barrels but they were utterly useless to him. Here was food enough, he reflected, if a man had teeth to gnaw through oak staves.

Now and again he had to cross to the other door which led into the cabin passageway and press his ear against a plank to make certain against surprise. Up and down the dark room he blundered, refusing to admit himself beaten. The first bit of cheer was when his foot struck a round object as solid as a round shot and he picked up a small Dutch cheese. This renewed his courage and he ransacked the corners on hands and knees. Blackbeard's treasure chest was not half so precious as a side of salted fish which he ran down by scent, saying to himself:

"With this rancid cheese and the slab o' ancient cod, ye could smell my course a league to wind'ard."

In a crumpled sack he found a few pounds of what seemed to be wheat flour, by the feel and taste of it. Poor stuff as it was, dry and uncooked, he added it to his stock.

"Rubbishy vittles," he sighed. "They may keep a man alive but he'll choke to death a-swallowin' of 'em."

Water was the desperate necessity and it was not to be sought for in the storeroom. There was rum enough, the place reeked with it, but to thirsty throats it was so much liquid fire. Joe was resolved not to return to Jack Cockrell without a few pints of water if reckless enterprise could procure it. Was the cabin still empty? He stood for a long time and listened but there was not a sound beyond the door of the passageway. Taking his courage in both hands he pushed at the door and it creaked open on rusty hinges. Light as a feather he moved one foot in front of the other, halted, advanced another step, and so entered the large cabin in which Stede Bonnet had lived with a Spartan simplicity.

What Joe coveted was the porous jar or water-monkey which hung suspended in a netting above the table. It was kept filled, he knew, in order to cool the tepid water from the casks. A heavenly sight it was to him to see the drops sweating on its rounded sides. He snatched it down and was about to make a swift retirement, but still spread upon the table he noted the chart of the Carolina and Virginia coasts which he had pored over with Stede Bonnet. This he delayed to roll up and tuck under one arm, not that he expected to employ it himself, but to make cruising more difficult for Blackbeard.

This bit of strategy held him a moment too long. He shot a glance over his shoulder, alarmed by a tread on the companion ladder. Horrified he beheld a pair of Spanish boots with scarlet, crinkled morocco tops, and they encased bandy legs which were strong and thick. What saved the miserable young Hawkridge was that the occupant of these splendid boots paused half-waydown the ladder to shout a profane command or two in those husky accents so feared by all lawful shipmen.

Before that sable beard came into his field of vision the lad was in full stride, running like a whippet, chart under one arm, water-jar under the other. He checked himself to ease the door behind him just as the truculent captor of the *Royal James* brig reached the foot of the ladder and let his gaze rove about the cabin. Sinking to the floor of the storeroom, Joe was afraid that for once he was about to swoon like a silly maid at sight of a mouse. As he had truly said, this pirating was no trade for a nervous man. Never mind, a miss was as good as a mile. Thankful for the darkness that closed around him, he slung the water-monkey over his shoulder in its hammock of netted cord, pushed the side of codfish inside his shirt, poked the chart into his boot-leg, put the cheese in the sack atop the flour, and was freighted for his journey through the hold.

This he accomplished after great difficulty and had to whistle and wait for a response before he could be sure of Jack Cockrell's whereabouts.

"What luck, Joe?" was the plaintive question. "I'd sooner starve than be left alone in this dungeon."

"Behold the dashing 'prentice-boy with another hairbreadth escape to his credit," replied the hero. "Be thankful for your dinner 'cause Blackbeard all but made a mouthful of me."

"You saw him, Joe"Up to the middle of him, and that was a-plenty. Don't ask me. I had a bad turn."

"I feel sick, too," said Jack. "The smell of this vile bilge-water breeds a nausea, and, whew, 'tis worse than ever."

"Bilge, my eye! You sniff the banquet I fetched ye. Here's a prime cheese that was hatched when Trimble Rogers was a pup."

Jack offered a feeble apology and felt revived after a pull at the water-monkey. What they craved most was a spark of light, the glimmer of a candle to lift this appalling gloom which pressed down like a visible burden. With nothing to do but discuss the situation from every slant and angle of conjecture, it was Joe Hawkridge's theory that Stede Bonnet would not rest content with regaining the *Revenge* but would come out to attack the brig as soon as the wind favored. His hatred of Blackbeard was one motive but there was a point of honor even more compelling.

"He called you his guest, Jack," explained Joe, "and I never did see a man so jealous of his plighted word when once he swore it. He took obligation to set you safe in Charles Town, d'ye see? And powder smoke won't stop him."

"Will Blackbeard tarry for a fight, Joe?"

"Not to my notion. He knows well this brig is no match for the *Revenge*, knows it better than did Cap'n Bonnet, what with all the heavy metal slung aboardfrom the sloop. And what does Blackbeard gain by having this brig hammered into a cocked hat? Fate tricked him comically with this swappin' about of ships."

"And will he linger on this coast? Oh, Joe, if he goes for a long cruise, what in mercy's name becomes of us two?"

"A long cruise, it looks like, shipmate. In the *Revenge* he could laugh at the small king's men-o'-war commissioned to hunt him down. He was ready to slap alongside any of 'em. Now 'tis different. As another flea in his ear, I stole the only chart of these waters. To the south'ard he'll turn, and I will bet that rampageous cheese on it."

"Clear to the Bay of Honduras?" said Jack.

"As far as that, at a guess. Or he may skirt the Floridas to look for Spanish prizes and put in at the Dry Tortugas which is a famous rendezvous for pirates of the Main. He will be hot to fit himself with a bigger ship, by capture or by some knavish trick such as he dealt Cap'n Bonnet."

CHAPTER XIV

BLACKBEARD APPEARS IN FIRE AND BRIMSTONE

HERE was a tragic predicament from which there was no release. Jack Cockrell was firmly convinced that Blackbeard must have recognized him that day in the swamp while Joe felt no less certain that he was marked for death because he had been one of the party of marooned mutineers. The hope of prolonging their existence by means of raiding the storeroom had ebbed after Joe's investigation. Such provisions as had been broken out of bulk were kept in lockers and pantries on deck where they were convenient to the galley and forecastle. It was realized also that their twittering nerves could not long withstand the darkness and suspense once the brig had put out to sea. Joe Hawkridge had nothing more to say about enduring it a month o' Sundays.

While the brig remained at anchor they clung to the thought that Captain Stede Bonnet might intervene in their behalf. It did bring them a gleam of solace to imagine him hoisting sail on the *Revenge* and crowding out to rake the brig with his formidable broadsides. And yet they were in doubt whether the *Revenge* was fit to proceed at once, what with all the work there hadbeen to do, rigging a new foremast, caulking leaky seams, repairing the other ravages of the storm.

These pitiable stowaways had no means of telling one hour from another until, at length, they heard over their heads the faint, musical strokes of the ship's bell on the forecastle head. This led them to believe that the fog had cleared else Blackbeard would not have revealed the vessel's position. And lifting fog meant a breeze to sweep it away from the harbor.

"Eight bells she strikes, the first o' the forenoon watch," said Joe. "We have been cooped in this black pit a matter of three hours a'ready."

"No more than that?" groaned Jack. "It seems at least a week. We must divert ourselves in some wise. What say if I learn you a bit o' Latin? And you can say over such sea songs as come to mind, for me to tuck in my memory."

"Well said, my worthy scholar. 'Tis high time we bowled ahead with my eddication as a proper gentleman."

Jack began to conjugate *amo, amas, amat*, and the pupil droned it after him but the verb *to love* recalled a black-eyed lass who had stolen his heart in the Azores and he veered from the Latin lesson to confide that sentimental passage. So Jack hammered nouns of the first declension into him until they grew tired of that, and then the sea waif played his part by reciting such fo'castle ballads as "*Neptune's Raging Fury, or The Gallant] Seaman's Sufferings,*" and "*Sir Walter Raleigh Sailing in the Lowlands.*"

This was better than the slow agony of waiting in silence, but Joe spoiled it by turning lovelorn and Jack bemourned fair Dorothy Stuart of Charles Town whom he would never greet again, and they sang very softly together a verse of "*The Maid's Lamentation*" which went like this:

"There shall be no Scarf go on my Head,
No Comb into my Hair,
No Fire burn, no Candle light
To shew my Beauty fair,
For never will I married be
Until the Day I die,

Since the Seas and the Winds
Has parted my Love and me."

This left them really in worse spirits than before, and they drowsed off
to sleep, and no wonder, after such a night as they had passed.
Accustomed to broken watches, Joe Hawkridge slept uneasily with one
ear open. Once or twice he sat up, heard Jack's steady snores, and lay
down again. It was the ship's bell which finally brought him to, and he
counted the strokes.

"Five bells, but what watch is it?" he muttered anxiously. "How long
was I napping? Lost track o' the time, so I have, and can't say if it's
night or day."

He sat blinking into the darkness and then had an inspiration. So
staunch and well-kept was the brig that the deck seams were tight and
no light filtered through. Joe left his hiding-place and groped along to
where he thought the main hatch ought to be. Gazing upward he saw a
gleam like a silvered line between the coaming and the edge of the
canvas cover which was battened with iron bars. This persuaded him
that the day had not yet faded, and he concluded that he had heard the
bell strike either in the afternoon watch or the second dog watch of
early evening.

This he imparted to Jack, after prodding him awake. They mulled it
over and agreed that Captain Bonnet must have found
the *Revenge* unready to weigh anchor or he would have engaged the brig
ere this. Perhaps there was not breeze enough for either vessel to move.
Another hour of this stressful tedium and they heard a sound of sharp
significance. It was the lap-lap of water against the vessel's side. No

more than the thickness of the planking was between them and this tinkling sea, and Joe exclaimed, in an agitated whisper:

"A breeze o' wind! Gentle it draws, but steady, like it comes off the land at sundown."

"The same as it did when we were blown offshore on the little raft, after we quitted the *Plymouth Adventure*," replied Jack.

"Blackbeard will take advantage of it to make for the open sea. There be three things offered us, Master Cockrell, to starve or go mad in this blighted hold, tosally on deck and beg mercy, which means a short shift, or to climb out softly in the night and try to swim for it."

"Swim to what, Joe?"

"Swim to the bottom, most likely. But we might fetch one o' them cays or the coast itself if he steers close in to find smooth water. 'Tis the worst odds yet but I'd sooner drown than tarry in this vessel. One miracle was wrought when the cask came driftin' to the beach to save me, and who knows but the Lord can spare another one for the salvation of us poor lads that mean to do right and forsake piratin'."

As they expected, there came soon the familiar racket of making sail and trimming yards and the clank of the capstan pawls. Then the anchor flukes scraped and banged against the bow timbers. The vessel heeled a little and the lapping water changed its tune to a swash-swash as the hull pushed it aside. The brig was alive and in motion.

"She makes no more than two or three knots," observed Joe, after a little while. "Ye can tell by the feel of her. The wind is steady but small."

"Then he can't go clear of the islands till long after night," thankfully returned Jack.

Joe made another trip to crane his neck at the main hatch. The bright thread of daylight had dimmed. He could scarce discern it. The lads occupied themselves with reckoning the distance, the hour, and the vessel's speed. Now that Joe had satisfied himself that the end of the day was near, he knew what the ship's bell meant when it was struck every half-hour. They would await the passing of another hour, until two bells of the first watch, by which time they calculated the brig should be in the wide, outer channel between the seaward islands.

The plan was to emerge through the forepeak in the very bows of the ship where a scuttle was let into the deck. There they might hope to lower themselves to the chain stays under the bowsprit and so drop into the sea. They would be washed past the ship, close to her side, and into the wake, and there was little chance of drawing attention. True it was that in this hard choice they preferred to swim to the bottom if so it had to be.

They crouched where they were hid, waiting to hear the fateful signal of two bells. It struck, mellow, clear, and they were about to creep in the direction of the forepeak. But Joe Hawkridge gripped his comrade's arm and held him fast. A whispered warning and they ceased to move. Behind them, in the after part of the ship, gleamed a lantern. It illumined the open door of the bulkhead which walled off the storeroom. And in this doorway, like a life-sized portrait, grotesque and sinister, set in a frame, was the figure of Blackbeard.

He advanced into the hold and the cowering stowaways assumed that he had come to search them out. The impulse was to dash into the forepeak and soplunge overboard, flinging away all caution, but before their palsied muscles could respond, the behavior of Blackbeard held them irresolute and curious. He had turned his back to them and was shouting boisterously to others to follow him. Seven men came through the doorway, one after the other, hanging back with evident reluctance. It was impossible to discern who they were, whether officers or seamen. Every one carried in his arms what looked to be a tub or an iron pot. These they set upon the dunnage boards which covered the ballast and made a flooring in the hold.

Blackbeard bellowed at them to squat in a circle, which they meekly did. He was in one of his fiendishly mirthful humors, rumpling his beard, strutting to and fro, laughing in senseless outbursts. At such times his men were most fearful for their lives. What sort of an infernal pastime he had now concocted was beyond the imagination of the lads who were concealed a dozen yards away. He was not hunting them, this much was plain, and it seemed wise to be quiet and avoid drawing attention to themselves.

They saw Blackbeard ignite a torch at the lantern and poke it into one pot after another. Flames began to burn, blue and green and yellow, and lurid smoke rolled to the deck-beams overhead. Amid this glare and reek of combustibles, Blackbeard waved his torch and tremendously proclaimed:

"Come, lads, we be all devils together, with a hell ofour own,— brimstone fires and pitch. Now, braggarts, see how long ye can bear it. 'Tis a foretaste of what's in store for all hands. At this game I'll outlast ye, for, harkee, I sold my soul to the Old Scratch as is well known."

HE LOOMED LIKE THE BELIAL WHOM HE WAS SO FOND OF CLAIMING AS HIS MENTOR

He stirred his infernal pots and the greasy smoke rolled upward in choking volume. The brimstone fumes were so vile and noxious that the victims of this outlandish revel soon gasped and wheezed. But they dared not object nor move from their places among the villainous pots. Blackbeard enjoyed their sufferings, taunting them as milksops and poltroons who could not endure even this taste of Gehenna. He himself appeared to be unaffected by it, lurching from one man to another, whacking them with the burning torch or playfully upsetting them. In the gaseous pall of smoke he loomed like the Belial whom he was so fond of claiming as his mentor.

Finally one of his involuntary guests toppled over in a faint. Blackbeard was kind enough to haul him to the door and boot him through it. A second man dragged himself thither. A third found voice to supplicate. The witch-fires still smoked and stewed in the pots and Blackbeard had proved that he was the toughest demon of them all.

The two stowaways watched this demented exploit in sheer wonderment. The fumes were not dense in their part of the hold and they could breathe, butthey well-nigh strangled in trying to refrain from coughing. The fires of tar and brimstone and what not cast so much light that they dared not betray themselves by crawling toward the forepeak. The upright beams between the keelson and the deck threw black shadows over them and they were in no great peril of detection so long as they stayed motionless.

Joe Hawkridge had heard gossip of this extraordinary amusement as a kind of initiation for hands newly joining Blackbeard's ship. He therefore read it that these unfortunates were some of Stede

Bonnet's men who had been captured with the brig. They had been allowed to enlist and were being taught to respect their new master.

Jack Cockrell had hugely admired young Joe for his ready wit and coolness in other crises of their mutual fortunes but now came a moment in which the astute sea urchin surpassed himself. It was not too much to say that he displayed absolute genius with the sturdy Master Cockrell to aid and abet him. Joe clawed in the dark until he found the sack with a few pounds of wheat flour in it. A quick whisper and his comrade grasped the great idea. They took no thought of a sequel. They would trust to opportunity. Hastily they rubbed the flour into their shirts and breeches. They covered their faces with it and lavishly sprinkled their hair. They looked at each other in the shadow of the beams and were pleased with their handiworkAnother whispered consultation and Joe possessed himself of the cannon-ball of a cheese while Jack grasped the side of salt-fish by the tail. They resembled two whitened clowns of a pantomime but in spirit they were as grimly serious as the menace of death could make them.

Blackbeard was dancing clumsily, like a drunken bear, and deriding with lewd oaths the two or three tortured survivors of his brimstone carnival. In a high, wailing voice which rose to a shriek there was borne to him the words:

"Ye dirked poor Jesse Strawn and left him rotting in the swamp. I was a true and faithful seaman, Cap'n Teach."

A deeper voice boomed out, filling the hold with unearthly echoes:

"I am the shade of the master mariner whom ye did foully murder off Matanzas and there is no rest for me ten fathom down."

The apparitions flitted out of the shadow and were vaguely disclosed in the flickering glare from the brimstone pots. The smoke gave them a wavering aspect as though their shapes were unsubstantial. Blackbeard stood beholding them in a trance of horror. With an aimless finger he traced the sign of the cross and his pallid lips moved in the murmur:

"The ghost o' Jesse Strawn! For the love of God, forbear

It was a petition as pious as ever Christian uttered. Forgotten was his wicked counterfeit of the nether region. Again the shrill voice wailed:

"Pity poor Jesse Strawn. I'll haunt ye by land and sea, Cap'n Teach. Swear by the Book to let that treasure chest lie at the bottom of the creek else I tear your sinful soul from your body."

The terrible Blackbeard was incapable of motion. Huskily he muttered:

"I'll ne'er seek the chest, good Jesse Strawn, an' it please you to pass me by."

The two spectres moved forward as the one of the deeper voice declaimed:

"Doomed I was to find no rest till I overtook your ship, Ed'ard Teach. Each night you'll see me walk the plank from your quarter-deck."

The unhappy Blackbeard gibbered something and would have fled as the spirits approached him. But those bandy legs tottered and before he could turn the awful visitants were upon him. One raised a round shot above his head, or so it appeared to be, and smote him full upon the crown. The other whirled a flat bludgeon and hit him on the jaw. With the smell of brimstone was mingled the pungent flavor of ripe cheese and salt-fish. Blackbeard measured his length, and the ghost of Jesse Strawn delayed an instant to dump a pot of sizzling combustibles over him.

Then the spirits twain made for the cabin at topspeed. Several of the crew had rushed down to harken to the strange disturbance. They scattered wildly at the first glimpse of these phantoms, being superstitious sailormen with many a wicked deed to answer for. It flashed into Joe Hawkridge's mind that all the men of the watch might be chased below, the hatches clapped on them, and the mastery of the brig secured. Blackbeard was absent for reasons best known to himself and his pirates lacked leadership. A brace of ghosts could put them to panic rout. And, no doubt, that wailing message of dead Jesse Strawn had carried like the cry of a banshee.

The poop was deserted in the twinkling of an eye, even to the pair of helmsmen and the officer of the watch. Against the sky of night the unwelcome phantoms were wan and luminous while the groans which issued from them were enough to curdle the blood of the brawniest pirate. He who had been Jack Cockrell in mortal guise was quick to slide the cabin hatch closed and fasten it. For the moment they had captured the armed brig *Royal James* and as ferocious a crew of rascals as ever scuttled a merchantman.

Joe Hawkridge glided to the taffrail and peered over the stern. A boat was towing behind the ship. It had been left there for taking soundings or pulling the brig's head around while she was still in the shoaler waters near the coast. This was better than Joe had dared anticipate. Feeling his way along the rail, he found theend of the rope which was belayed around a wooden pin. Heaven be praised, they would not have to swim for it! He beckoned his comrade to say in his ear:

"They will soon find their wits. It 'ud be foolish to try scaring 'em under hatches now that the jolly-boat floats so handy. There's hard cases amongst 'em that will begin shooting at us presently. Down the rope ye go, Jack. I'll stand by and give 'em another dose of poor Jesse Strawn."

Over the rail flew the stouter phantom of the two and slid like a white streak, fetching up in the boat with a most earthly and substantial thump. With a farewell wail the other ghost flung a limber leg over and shot down so fast that his hands were scorched. To such pirates as beheld this instant vanishment, these disturbing spirits floated off into space. Jack cut the rope with his knife and the boat dropped back in the shining wake. They shoved out two heavy oars and fairly broke their hearts in pulling dead into the wind where the brig would have to tack to pursue them.

The rattle of the oars and the discovery of the shorn rope's end must have convinced the pirates who ran aft that they had been tricked by mortal beings like themselves. A musket spat a red streak of fire. Blocks whined as the braces were hauled to change the brig's course. In the light breeze she responded awkwardly and soon hung in stays. Meanwhile the jolly-boat was slowly working to windward while two frightened ladstugged and swung until the flour turned to paste on their dripping faces.

Before the brig began to forge ahead, the boat was invisible from her decks. This was evident because the spatter of musket-fire ceased. Soon the fugitives heard Blackbeard's harsh voice damning all hands. That thick skull of his had not been cracked by the impact of the solid cheese and he had been released from his brimstone inferno. The ghosts rested on their oars. They could watch the glimmering canvas of the brig and see what her procedure might be. Soon she filled away and forsook the attempt to find the boat. Blackbeard had wisdom enough to avoid blundering about and putting the brig aground in a chase so elusive as this.

"Farewell, ye hairy son of Tophet," said Joe Hawkridge, waving his hand at the disappearing vessel. "And here's hoping I set your whiskers ablaze when I turned the pot over 'em."

"Did you hear him swear not to touch the treasure chest, Joe? That was a master stroke of yours."

"Aye, it was bright of me. But he thinks different now. He knows we made a booby of him."

"But we learned one thing,—he hasn't recovered the treasure yet," suggested Jack.

"He is such a powerful liar that I don't know as the ghost o' Jesse Strawn could budge the truth out of him. However, it was comfortin' to hear him swear it on his marrow-bones. I fetched away the navigation chart the one I poached from the cabin table. It gives us the lay o' the coast."

"What ho and whither bound?" was Jack's question. "Here is a sail wound round a sprit beneath the thwarts."

"The wrong wind to head for Cap'n Bonnet and the *Revenge*. This swag-bellied jolly-boat handles like a firkin. We had best wait for day and then decide the voyage."

"Nothing to eat and no water, Joe. All I can find is an empty pannikin."

"You're a glutton," severely exclaimed young Hawkridge. "After the banquet I served in the hold!"

What Master Cockrell said in reply sounds as familiar and as wistful to-day as when he spoke it two hundred years ago.

"I have had enough of wandering and strange adventures, Joe. I want to go home."

CHAPTER XV

MR. PETER FORBES MOURNS HIS NEPHEW

IT seems a long time, in the course of this story, since the honorable Secretary of the Council, Mr. Peter Arbuthnot Forbes, was forced to sail in to Charles Town from the *Plymouth Adventure* on that most humiliating errand of finding medicines for Blackbeard's fever-smitten rogues. For the sake of his own dear nephew and the other hostages detained on board, he had endeavored to perform his bargain and was returning across the bar when the threatening clouds and other portents of a violent storm caused the seamen to lose heart. They put about and drove back into the harbor for shelter in the very nick of time.

These were pirates from Blackbeard's crew, it may be recalled, with his grizzled, scarred boatswain at the tiller. They had felt safe enough to swagger and ruffle it through the streets of Charles Town and to terrify the people. Their worthless lives were protected by the hostages who waited in fear and trembling. The town seethed with indignation and was hot with shame. There would be no more of the friendly traffic with pirates.

It was fully believed that the wretched Blackbeardwould be as good as his word in allowing no more than two days' grace. Therefore when Mr. Peter Forbes came back in the boat to inform his neighbors that he had been unable to reach the ship, it was sadly taken for granted that those helpless passengers had been put to death. Forthwith the pirates of the boat's crew were seized and thrown in gaol. There they lay in double irons until the Council met and ordered them to be tried. In accordance with the verdict the six seamen and the boatswain were promptly hanged by the neck from the same gallows at White Point hard by the town. And the people no longer shivered at the name of Blackbeard nor feared his vengeance. Their fighting blood was thoroughly aroused.

Not long after this, there arrived from England a new Governor of the Province, a man of honor and resolution who approved what had been done. This Governor Johnson proceeded to organize the town for defense, building batteries on Sullivan's Island, recruiting the seafaring men in the militia, and seeking to obtain merchant vessels which could be employed as armed cruisers. Learning that the Governor of North Carolina was in a corrupt partnership with pirates, he sent messages to Virginia to solicit coöperation.

This activity made much work for Secretary Peter Forbes who forsook his intention of going to England to beg the coöperation of his Majesty's Government against the plague of pirates. Dapper and plump and important as of yore, his florid face was clouded with sorrow and he seemed a much older man. He mourned his nephew, Jack Cockrell, as no more and felt as though he had lost an only son. Every angry word he had ever addressed the lad, every hasty punishment inflicted, hurt him grievously.

It was a solace to talk with winsome Dorothy Stuart because hers was the bright optimism of youth and she held so exalted an opinion of Jack's strength and courage that she refused to abandon hope. And the fact that he had confided to her his rash intention of running away and signing as a pirate sooner than be transported to school in England, persuaded her that he might be alive.

"From what you saw yourself, Mr. Forbes," said she, "when Blackbeard boarded the *Plymouth Adventure* with his dreadful men, our Jack won his fancy."

"So it appeared, Dorothy. The boy boasted of knocking a tall pirate on the head, and he read this monster of a pirate more shrewdly than I. Yes, Blackbeard took it with rough good humor. But Jack would ne'er consent to sail with him. 'Twas that confounded Stede Bonnet with his gallant air that turned the lad's head. He cast a glamor over this trade of murder and pillage."

"Be that as it may," returned Dorothy, with a sigh and a smile, "I confess to a romantic admiration for this bold Captain Bonnet. He wears an air of mystery which is most becoming. We must not blame poor Jack."

"No, no, I am done with all that," hastily exclaimed Uncle Peter. "All I dare hope is that when Blackbeard is captured, we may learn what fate befell the boy. It makes the torture worse to have him vanish without trace."

"And yet I have faith the sea will give him back to us, Mr. Forbes. He will find you a chastened guardian, not so apt to box his ears."

Uncle Peter was so distressed by this gentle raillery that the girl begged pardon and vowed that she would never again offend. It so happened that they were sitting together in Parson Throckmorton's garden a day or so after this when a friend came running in with tidings the most unexpected and incredible. A negro slave had come from a plantation a few miles inland and he bore a letter written by none other than Captain Jonathan Wellsby of the *Plymouth Adventure*. It narrated how he and the survivors of his ship had journeyed that far after weeks of suffering and frequent skirmishes with Indians. They were compelled to rest and take shelter before undertaking the last stage of the journey.

Councilor Peter Forbes was magically changed. He shed his dignity and threw his hat in air. Clasping Miss Dorothy's slender waist, he planted a kiss on her damask cheek. Parson Throckmorton was ramming snuff intohis nostrils, his wig all awry, while he sneezed trumpet blasts of rejoicing.

"Survivors? *Kerchooh!* God bless me, that lusty stripling will be amongst them,—*kerchooh,*—he can survive anything but Greek and Latin,—*kerchooh,*—I will spare the rod in future."

"I told you so, Uncle Peter Forbes," laughed Dorothy.

"Not so fast," quoth he, in a mood suddenly sobered. "Captain Wellsby includes no list of those in his party."

"But, of course, one of them is *sure* to be Master Jack," she insisted.

"I am a selfish man and a laggard officer of the Crown," he exclaimed with air of great self-reproach. "There are women in that company and wounded men, no doubt. We must take them clothing, horses, food, a surgeon."

He bustled off to the Governor's house to find that energetic gentleman absent at Sullivan's Island. Acting for him, the Secretary of the Council sent the town crier to summon all good citizens to the tavern green. In the space of an hour the men and supplies were assembled and with Mr. Forbes in command the band of mercy made haste to reach the plantation. During the march there was a buzz of anxious surmise. Was this one and that alive or dead? Had

the hostages been slain and were these the sailormen of
the *PlymouthAdventure* who had been set adrift by Blackbeard?
Councilor Forbes winced at hearing such talk as this, but his heart
beat high nevertheless, so confident was he that he was about to
behold his manly nephew.

There was loud cheering when they came to the cleared land of the
indigo fields and saw a tattered British ensign fluttering from the
log stockade which enclosed the huts of the overseer and his
laborers. In the gateway appeared the stalwart figure of Captain
Wellsby in ragged garments and with a limping gait. Other men
crowded behind him and responded with huzzas which were like a
feeble echo. The friends from Charles Town rushed forward to
embrace them, loudly demanding to know where the rest were.

"We fetched the women safe through," answered Captain Wellsby
whose eyes were sunken and the brown beard streaked with gray.
"Twelve good men of my crew are dead, and three of the
gentlemen passengers. The swamps took toll of some and the
Indians slew the others. We were besieged a fortnight by the
Yemassees,—a hard experience all of it, and wondrous luck to have
escaped——"

Councilor Forbes delayed while his companions entered the huts to
attend the invalids. He struggled to ask a question but his voice was
beyond control.

"I understand," kindly spoke the shipmaster. "Your lad is not with
us, nor can I say if he be dead or alive

"The Indians carried him off?" weakly inquired the uncle.

"No, he was never seen after we abandoned ship. Your Jack and a chum of his from Blackbeard's crew were for making the beach on a small raft of their own contrivance. This was after nightfall, Councilor, and what with a land'ard breeze and a crotchety set of the tide amongst the shoals, they floated out to sea."

"On a small raft," muttered Mr. Forbes, "and a vast ocean. I know of no ship voyaging to or from these ports which might have found them."

"I was in hopes of hearing news of the lads from you," sorrowfully said the shipmaster. "There is the chance, tiny though it be, that they were sighted by some vessel bound to foreign parts, across the Western Ocean."

The uncle shook his head in a manner profoundly dejected. There were duties which summoned him and he choked down his own grief, turning from the sympathetic mariner to minister to those in distress. Horse litters were soon ready for the exhausted but heroic women who had been kept alive by the devotion of the noble British seamen in accordance with the traditions of the merchant service. Those unable to walk farther were placed in carts. Clothed and fed, the sailors were in blithe spirits and talked of going to sea again as soon as they could find a ship.

In the crowd which met them on the outskirts of theCharles Town settlement was Dorothy Stuart. She scanned the straggling column and then ran from one cart to another. It was impossible to convince her that Jack Cockrell was not there. But when she heard from Uncle Peter the news that Jack was missing but not surely dead, her faith burned anew, triumphant over fact and reason.

"See how the great storm came to save him from Blackbeard," she cried, her hand nestling in Uncle Peter's arm. "And look how he came unscathed through that bloody battle with the pirates in the *Plymouth Adventure*. Why, a cruise on a raft is merely a frolic after all that."

"I would not discourage your dear dreams, sweet maid," was the gentle response. "And may they be truer than my own forebodings."

Charles Town was more than ever resentful when it learned from these poor people how the pirate sailing-master, Ned Rackham, had plotted to get rid of them and how mournful had been their sufferings after the shipwreck. The one boat left to them had been too rotten to send along the coast and they had plunged into a wilderness almost impassable.

Meanwhile Governor Johnson, stirred by this episode, had received word that the province of Virginia was both ready and anxious to join in an expedition against Blackbeard. Governor Spottswood of Virginia would be outfitting such craft as he could get together in theJames River while he awaited a reinforcement from Charles Town.

The best vessel available for immediate use was a small brigantine, the *King George*. There was no lack of eager seamen when Councilor Forbes and Colonel Stuart proclaimed the muster on the tavern green. Among those selected were several of Captain Jonathan Wellsby's sailors who were primed to fight even though there was not much flesh on their bones. He himself was a forlorn mariner who had lost his good ship and found no joy in life. With a grim smile of gratitude he accepted the invitation to go as master of the *King George*, with Colonel Stuart as a sea soldier to drill the men and lead them in action.

It was while they were slinging guns aboard the brigantine that some of the men happened to notice a small boat coming into the harbor under a rag of sail. At first it was taken for a fishing craft and there was no comment until it was quite close. Then they saw that it was a ship's jolly-boat much the worse for wear, with only two occupants. These were half-naked lads, burned black to the waist, with a queer kind of canvas head-gear as a protection against the sun.

The boat was steered to pass under the stern of the *King George* and the crew was unable to fathom if these were pirates or victims of another shipwreck. Captain Wellsby solved it by shouting:

"Both your guesses are right! One is the pirateyounker that served our cause in the *Plymouth Adventure* and t'other is Master Jack Cockrell!"

One of the Charles Town volunteers heard only the word *pirate* and growled, with an oath:

"One o' Blackbeard's spawn? We'll make precious short work of him. Hand me a musket and I will save trouble for the hangman."

"Here, stop that," said Captain Wellsby, beckoning his own men. "You old *Adventure* hands know better. Quell these lubbers. If there's to be hostile feeling ashore I shall take this lad aboard under my own protection."

During this argument the sea-worn pilgrims in the jolly-boat had recognized the shipmaster and were joyfully yelling at him. In response to his gesture, they pulled down the sail and rowed to the gangway of the brigantine. There was no need to fear the wrath of the Charles Town seamen, because the *Adventure* hands stood by as a guard while they explained how this young Joe Hawkridge had valiantly helped to turn the tide of battle against the prize crew of pirates. And there was such a rousing welcome for Master Cockrell that all else was forgotten. His old shipmates fairly mobbed him.

"I will fire a gun and hoist all the bunting to signal the town," cried the skipper, his face shining. "And presently I'll send you to the wharf in my own boat, but first tell me, boys, who took you off the little raft and whence come you in this ship's boat"Blackbeard rescued us. And we borrowed the boat from him," demurely answered Jack, watching the effect of this bombshell of a sensation.

"*Blackbeard!*" echoed the bedazed shipmaster and the others chimed it like a chorus.

"Aye, old Buckets o' Blood hisself," grinned Joe Hawkridge. "We had him tamed proper when we parted company. First we chased him through a swamp till his tongue hung out and left him mired to the whiskers. Then for another lark we scared him in his own ship so he begged us on his knees to forbear. We learned Cap'n Ed'ard Teach his manners, eh, Jack?"

This was too much for the audience which stood agape. A dozen voices at once implored enlightenment. With a lordly air for a youth whose costume was mostly one leg of his breeches, Master Cockrell reproved them to wit:

"Captain Stede Bonnet was more courteous to our distress when we sailed with him. He gave us a thumping big breakfast."

"Right-o," declared Joe. "'Tis our custom to spin strange yarns for clothes and vittles in payment."

The men scampered to the galley and pantry but refused to let Captain Wellsby carry these rare entertainers into the cabin. Graciously they sketched the chief events, omitting all mention of the treasure chest, and Jack explained in conclusion

"And so I was stricken homesick, like an illness, and Joe had his fill of pirates, too. The wind was wrong to rejoin Captain Bonnet in the Inlet harbor after we shipped as ghosts in the jolly-boat, and we had a mariner's chart of the Carolina coast and——"

"But what did you do for subsistence?" broke in Captain Wellsby.

"Food and water?" answered Joe. "Oh, we landed when the thirst plagued us too bad. And there was rain to fill a bight of the sail and a pannikin to save it in."

"And we lived on oysters mostly," said Jack, "and Joe killed a fat opossum with a club, and we caught some fish in a net which I knotted from a ball of marline that was in the boat. And we foraged for pawpaws and persimmons."

"And whenever the breeze was fair we put to sea again," said Joe, "and it was a long and weary voyage, though not so many leagues on the chart."

The captain's boat was ready and they tumbled in, two wayfarers of the sea who were as lean and sun-dried as the buccaneers of old

Trimble Rogers' fond memories. Hardships had seasoned and weathered them like good ash staves. On the wharf was Uncle Peter Forbes and Governor Johnson and a concourse of townspeople drawn by the joyous signals flown from the brigantine. Jack looked in vain for Dorothy Stuart and was thankful that her welcome was deferred. Shears and a razorand Christian raiment would make him look less like a savage from the coast of Barbary.

Uncle Peter wasted a vast deal of pity, thinking the castaways too weak and wasted to walk. Jack strode along with him, the crowd at their heels, and soon had the plump Councilor puffing for breath. They insisted on taking Joe Hawkridge with them although he was for seeking lodgings at the tavern. He was one of the household, declared Mr. Forbes, while Jack warned him to beware of impertinence lest he be sentenced to chop wood for the kitchen fire.

The neighbors and friends, as curious as they were joyful, were barred from the house while the lads talked and Uncle Peter carefully made notes of it all. It was too much for him to realize that Jack was sitting there lusty and laughing and with the dutifully respectful manner as of yore, in spite of the man's part he had played to the hilt. Of all the exploits, that which most fascinated Mr. Peter Forbes was the chase after Blackbeard's sea-chest weighty with treasure and the discovery of the knoll in the Cherokee swamp where he might have buried other booty. Here was a picaresque romance which allured the methodical barrister and Councilor and he was as boyishly excited as his nephew. He examined the chart which Jack had copied from his rude sketch made on a piece of bark and this raised a question which he was quick to ask:

"What of Bill Saxby and this old bloodhound of a Trimble Rogers? As soon as Stede Bonnet could get the *Revenge* to sea, I have no doubt he sailed to Cape Fear River to get these pirate comrades of yours and the seamen he left to find them. Once aboard, they would urge Bonnet to return to Cherokee Inlet and let them go hunt the treasure."

"That may be, but we can trust them to deal fair by us," replied Jack.

"Possibly," was the skeptical comment. Mr. Forbes was not too ready to believe in honest pirates.

"I'm not sure Cap'n Bonnet had a mind to bother with this treasure hunting," suggested Joe Hawkridge. "Leastwise, he may ha' put it off to an easier day. He has friends that keep him well informed, such as the Governor of North Carolina at Bath Town. And all this flurry against piratin', here and in Virginia, 'ud be apt to make Cap'n Bonnet wary of bein' trapped on the coast."

"Joe is full of wisdom, as usual," said Master Cockrell. "And if Blackbeard has cruised to the Spanish Main, as we suspect, the treasure may lie undisturbed for a while."

"Concerning Blackbeard, the evidence then in hand warranted your conclusions," was Uncle Peter's judicial comment, "but I have received later information. The rumor is, and well-founded, that he turned his ship and made for the Pamlico River with the intention of obtaining pardon from the false and greedy Governor EdenThis would baffle our plans against him, or so he would assume. And it would enable him to remain within convenient distance of his treasure."

"Would this Province and Virginia respect such a pardon as that?" queried Jack.

"Not in the case of Blackbeard," snapped the Councilor, "because we know it would be violated as soon as this treacherous villain could safely return to his piracies."

"Then Joe and I will enlist in the *King George* brigantine," cried Jack. "Captain Wellsby tells me she will sail for Virginia inside the week."

Uncle Peter was about to make violent protest but he checked himself and his emotions were torn betwixt pride and yearning affection. He could not bear to let his nephew go so soon to new perils, but what right had he to try to shield him when the public duty called? It was idle to pretend that Jack was too young and tender to embark on such service as this. He was fitter for it than some of the other volunteers. And so the unhappy Uncle Peter walked the floor with his cheeks puffed out and his hands clasped behind him and said, with a tremulous sigh:

"I swore to treat you no more as a child, Jack. 'Tis right and natural for you to desire to go in the *King George* as a fighting man tried and true. As for Joe Hawkridge, I have acquainted the Governor with his merits and his pardon is assured

"Thankee, sir," returned the reformed young pirate. "A respectable life is what I crave, and the parson for company."

"It sounds almost pleasant to me, including the parson," admitted Jack, "as soon as we shall have settled this matter with Blackbeard."

CHAPTER XVI

NED RACKHAM'S PLANS GO MUCH AMISS

THE armed brigantine had been out several days on the voyage to Virginia when a vessel was sighted hull-down. Captain Wellsby and Colonel Stuart decided to edge over and take a look at the stranger although they were not anxious to engage an enemy of heavier metal. If, however, this should happen to be Blackbeard in the *Revenge* they were in no mood to avoid him, despite the odds. After an hour of sailing in a strong breeze, it was seen that this other vessel was a small merchantman which shifted her course as though to shake off pursuit.

"They take us for a pirate," chuckled Captain Wellsby. "I have no wish to scare 'em, poor souls. They will feel easy as soon as we bring the wind abeam."

He was about to give the order when Joe Hawkridge, gunner's mate, called to Jack Cockrell standing his watch at the helm:

"Remember the snow I told ye of? Yonder is the same rig and tonnage, alike it as peas in a pod."

Jack spoke to the shipmaster who summoned Joe to the quarter-deck. The boy was confident that this was the New England coasting vessel in which Ned Rackham and his pirates had appeared off Cherokee Inlet and had carried the marooned seamen from the sandy cay.

"A brown patch in the big main-topsail, and the bowsprit steeved more'n ordinary," said Joe. "Tit for tat, Cap'n Wellsby. Your men can have the fun of jamming them in the fo'castle. And you won't find me or Jack helpin' these picaroons to break out."

"No fear of that," sternly spoke the shipmaster. "They shall make their exit with a taut rope and a long drop when I deliver them in Virginia."

It was to be gathered that the bold Ned Rackham had failed in his desperate enterprise of capturing a larger ship and that he was probably cruising up the coast in hopes of rejoining Blackbeard. The snow had too few guns to cope with the *King George* brigantine which could throw a battering broadside. As soon as identification was certain, Captain Wellsby hauled to windward to hold the weather gauge and Colonel Stuart called the men to quarters. The *Plymouth Adventure* hands were disappointed that they would be unable to pay their own grudge. They had no doubt that Ned Rackham would strike his colors without a battle.

The *King George* ran close enough for Captain Wellsby to shout through the trumpet:

"The snow ahoy! Send your men aboard or I'll sink you. No tricks, Rackham. Lively, now."

They saw the men running to cut the boat lashingsand struggle to launch the boats from the deck. Ned Rackham, handsome and debonair, stared coolly at the brigantine but gave no sign that he had heard the ultimatum. With a shrug he walked across the poop, glanced up at the British ensign which flew from his main truck, and made no motion to pull it down.

"Blow your matches, boys," roared Colonel Stuart from his station in the waist of the *King George*. "Five minutes' grace, no more."

Captain Wellsby said to wait a little. The pirates were endeavoring to quit the snow. And presently Rackham appeared to change his own purpose. No longer ignoring the *King George*, he doffed his hat in a graceful flourish and bowed with a mocking obeisance. Then he strolled to the cabin hatch and went below, presumably to get a change of clothing or something of the sort. But he failed to reappear and his men were in a frenzy of haste, with one boat already in the water.

So incensed was Colonel Stuart by the insolent refusal of Ned Rackham to strike his colors in token of surrender that he gave orders to fire at the mainmast and try to bring it down. An instant before the starboard battery thundered, the snow seemed to fly upwards in a tremendous explosion. The masts were flung out of her and the hull opened like a shattered basket. So violent was the shock that men were thrown to the deck of the *King George* and she quivered as thoughher bows had rammed a reef. Black smoke spouted as from a crater and debris rained down on a boiling sea.

A few survivors, scorched or half-stunned, were clinging to bits of wreckage and wailing for succor. Where the snow had floated was a discolored eddy, broken timbers, a lather of dirty foam. Captain Jonathan Wellsby picked himself up, rubbed a bump on his head, and gazed wildly at the tragic scene. Collecting his wits, he exclaimed:

"That 'ud be like Ned Rackham, to blow up the ship sooner than be taken and hanged. More than likely he had the train all laid to the powder barrels."

"He saved us a lot of trouble," said Colonel Stuart as he climbed to the poop. "A fellow of iron will and courage, this Rackham, by all accounts. I have conceived a respect for him."

"I forgive him his sins," replied the skipper. "Now, lads, boats away, and fish up those dying wretches."

Joe Hawkridge emitted a jubilant whoop and dived over the rail without waiting for a boat. He had caught a glimpse of a feeble swimmer whose square, solid features and bushy brows were familiar. It was Peter Tobey, the carpenter's mate, who had befriended him on the cay and who had set adrift that miraculous cask of food and water. A few strokes and Joe was at his side, clutching him by the neck-band and towing him toward the *King George* like a faithful retriever. Ropes wereflung to them and Joe saw his good friend safely aboard before he went up the side.

The carpenter's mate was both burned and bruised but his hurts were not grievous and he was able to drag himself aft with Joe as a crutch.

"My own particular prize, sir, by your gracious leave," said Joe Hawkridge, addressing Captain Wellsby. "This is Mr. Peter Tobey, a poor, faint-hearted pirate like me. May I have him to keep, sir?"

"Bless me, but there will be no pirates left to hang," was the quizzical reply. "Master Cockrell has adopted you, and now I am ordered to be kind to Bill Saxby and Trimble Rogers if I meet up with 'em."

"That's the whole list, sir. Ask Jack Cockrell. You can string the rest of the bloody pirates to the yardarm, for all we care. Do I get exemption for this Peter Tobey?"

"What is your verdict, Colonel Stuart?" asked the captain.

"I heard the tale from Hawkridge," answered the brusque but generous soldier. "The carpenter's mate has won my allegiance. What say you in your own behalf, Peter Tobey?"

The blistered, singed survivor touched a hand to his forehead and respectfully responded:

"A carpenter by trade and nature, and allus was. I never see one happy day a-piratin' nor did I shed the blood of any human creatur'. With a bench and tools, you will find me a proper handy man in Charles Town."

"That clinches it," cried Colonel Stuart. "I should call it a crime to hang an artisan like Peter Tobey. Your prize is awarded you, Hawkridge. See that he is well cared for."

"The first booty that ever was handed me from a sinkin' ship," said Joe. "Come along, Master Tobey, and roll into my bunk."

"Verily I was castin' bread upon the waters when I gave that cask to the wind and tide," devoutly murmured the carpenter's mate as he limped below with his new owner.

No more than a dozen other pirates were rescued alive and several of these expired soon after they were lifted aboard the brigantine. This was the only sensational incident of the coastwise voyage to the James River. Comfortably quartered, with no more work than was wholesome, Jack Cockrell and Joe Hawkridge thought it a holiday excursion after their previous adventures at sea.

In the roadstead of the James were two men-of-war, small frigates flying the broad pennant of the Royal Navy. A conference was held in the cabin of the senior officer, to which Captain Wellsby and Colonel Stuart were invited. The latest advices made it seem certain that Blackbeard still lurked off the coast of the Carolinas. Planters had reported seeing his ship in Pamlico Sound and it was also learned that he had been in communication with the disloyal Governor Eden at Bath Town. A letter had been intercepted, in handwriting of the Governor's secretary, and addressed to Captain Teach, which included these words:

"I have sent you four of your men. They are all I can meet with about town. Be upon your guard."

This was readily construed to mean that Blackbeard was in haste to recall such of his crew as had strayed ashore. At the council of war in the frigate's cabin, a proclamation was read. It offered a handsome reward for the capture of Captain Edward Teach, dead or alive, and lesser rewards for other pirates.

It was the decision that the two frigates were unhandy for cruising inshore. Therefore officers and men would be chosen from them to fill the complements of two sloops, light and active craft which would be unhampered by batteries of cannon. They would be employed for boarding Blackbeard's ship while the Charles Town brigantine *King George* should convoy them and engage in the attack if the depth of water should permit. The naval officer selected to command the sloops was Lieutenant Maynard who went off to the *King George* to inspect her and make a call of courtesy.

He was especially cordial to Master Cockrell and Gunner's Mate Joe Hawkridge, laying aside the stiff dignity of naval rank. To his persuasive argument thatthey enter the royal service with promise of quick promotion, they turned a deaf ear although they were wonderfully taken with him. He was a gentle, soft-spoken young man with a boyish smile who blushed when pressed to talk of his own exploits against the Spanish, the Dutch, and the French in Britannia's wooden walls. His own questions were mostly about Blackbeard's fighting quality. Would he make a stand against disciplined tars who were accustomed to close in, hammer-and-tongs? Joe Hawkridge answered to this:

"I ne'er saw him in action against a king's ship, and all his wild nonsense is apt to delude ye into thinkin' him a drunken play-actor. But you will never take him alive, so long as those bandy legs have strength to prop him up."

"I look forward to meeting him with a deal of pleasure. It may be my good fortune to measure swords with him," observed Lieutenant Maynard.

Joe Hawkridge was puzzled by this gentle fire-eater with the complexion of a girl. Nothing could have been more unlike the ramping, roaring pirates of Blackbeard's dirty crew who tried to terrify by their very appearance. After the lieutenant had returned to his frigate, Jack Cockrell remarked:

"A most misleading man, Joe. You cannot picture him seeking the bubble reputation at the cannon's mouth, as Will Shakespeare saith."

"Blackbeard will bite him in two," replied Joe. "Heis too pretty to be risked in such a slaughter pen. I own up to feelin' squeamish on my own account, hardy pirate though I be."

"This Lieutenant Maynard is welcome to measure swords with Blackbeard," said Jack, "and I shall not quarrel with him for the honor. Pick me a pirate with a wooden leg, Joe, or one that still shakes with Spanish fever."

"My only chance of getting out with a whole skin is to lug a sack of flour under one arm and play the ghost o' Jesse Strawn."

Expeditiously the brigantine and the two sloops sailed out of the James River to head for the North Carolina coast and first rake the nooks and bays of Pamlico Sound. There was no intention of offering Blackbeard fair odds in battle. With men and vessels enough it was resolved to exterminate him, like ridding a house of rats or other vermin. If he had gone out to sea, then the pursuers would wait and watch for his return to his favorite haunts in these waters. There was every reason to believe, however, that he was concealed inshore, within easy distance of his friend Governor Eden.

Failing to find him in Pamlico Sound, it was debated whether to cruise farther to the southward. Now Master Jack Cockrell and his chum had said nothing to the officers concerning the treasure in the Cherokee swamp. They felt bound in honor not to reveal it without the consent of Bill Saxby and old Trimble Rogers who werepartners in the enterprise. Moreover, Lieutenant Maynard and the Virginia officers would feel bound to turn the treasure over to the crown or its representatives. Governor Eden of North Carolina would undoubtedly claim it as found within his territory and this meant that he would steal most of it for himself.

It thrilled the lads when Colonel Stuart told them that this Provincial squadron would cruise as far as Cherokee Inlet before working to the northward again. Information had led the officers to believe that Blackbeard had lost many men by desertion while his ship lay at Bath Town and near by. They had been roving about the plantations and making a nuisance of themselves and seemed ready to quit their red-handed despot of a master. In this event he might have sought his old hiding-place at the Inlet sooner than risk a clash with the force which had been sent after him and of which he had been warned by Governor Eden.

Lieutenant Maynard scouted in advance with the two sloops because there was small danger of their getting aground and they could be moved along with oars if the wind failed. The brigantine kept further offshore but within signaling distance. She was running within sight of the scattering barrier of low islands when Captain Wellsby summoned Joe Hawkridge and informed him:

"You will act as pilot, Joe, once we fetch sounding on the Twelve Fathom Bank. The chart is faulty, as yeknow, and me and my mates are in strange waters with a'mighty little elbow-room. You know the marks, I take it."

"Aye, sir, I do that," answered Joe. "Then I stays aboard ship and miss the chance to go pokin' about with a cutlass? I'm all screwed up to terrible deeds, Cap'n Wellsby, after a spell o' mortal fear. And who takes care of Master Cockrell if he goes in a boat?"

"His own lusty right arm, Joe. Avast with your melancholy. We must first catch this Blackbeard."

Presently Joe Hawkridge footed it up the main shrouds to scan the sea ahead and try to get a glimpse of that sandy bit of exposed shoal on which he had been marooned. This would enable him to find the entrance to the outer channel and so con the brigantine in from seaward. While he shaded his eyes with his hand against the glare of the morning sun, one of the sloops hoisted a string of bright signal flags and fired two guns. The other sloop was seen to lower her topsail and wait for the *King George* to come up.

Joe Hawkridge climbed higher and found a perch where he could discern the spars of a vessel etched almost as fine as threads against the azure horizon. He was almost certain that the ship he saw was very close to that tiny cay of which he had such unhappy knowledge. Soon he was able to perceive that the vessel's sails were furled. This was an odd place for an anchorage. His conjecture was confirmed when the *King George* passed close to the nearest sloop and Lieutenant Maynard shouted:

"Stranded hard and fast! And she is deucedly like Blackbeard's brig."

Scampering to the deck, Joe Hawkridge mustered his gun's crew as Jack Cockrell came running up to say:

"Trapped on the very islet where he cast you and the other pirates! His chickens have come home to roost."

"Call me no pirate or I'll stretch ye with a handspike," grinned Joe. "'Tis a plaguey poor word in this company. Aye, Cap'n Ed'ard Teach has a taste of his own medicine and he will get a worse dose this day than ever he served me."

CHAPTER XVII

THE GREAT FIGHT OF CAPTAIN TEACH

YES, there was Blackbeard's ship hard in the sand which had gripped her keel while she was steering to enter the Cherokee Inlet. There was no pearly vapor of swamp mist out here to shroud her from attack. The air was clear and bright, with a robust breeze which stirred a flashing surf on the shoals. Under lower sails, the two sloops watchfully crept nearer until their crews could examine the stranded brig and read the story of her plight. She stood on a slant with the decks sloped toward the enemy. This made it impossible to use her guns with any great effect.

Captain Wellsby tacked ship and kept the *King George* well away from the cay, as Joe Hawkridge advised. With an ebbing tide, it was unsafe to venture into shallower water in order to pound Blackbeard's vessel with broadsides. Lieutenant Maynard came aboard in a small boat and was quite the dandy with his brocaded coat and ruffles and velvet small-clothes. One might have thought he had engaged to dance the minuet. Colonel Stuart met him in a spick-and-span uniform of His Majesty's Foot, cross-belts pipe-clayed white as snow, boots polished until they shone. Such gentlemen were punctilious in war two hundred years ago.

"Your solid shot will not pound him much at this range, my good sir," said the lieutenant. "With his hull so badly listed toward us, you can no more than splinter the decks while his men take shelter below."

"I grant you that," regretfully replied the soldier. "And case-shot will not scatter to do him much harm. Shall I blaze away and demoralize the rascals whilst you make ready your boats?"

"Toss a few rounds into the varlets, Colonel Stuart. It may keep them from massing on deck. One boat from your ship, if it please you, with twenty picked men. I shall take twenty men from each sloop as boarders."

"Sixty in all?" queried the colonel. "Why not take a hundred?"

"They would be tumbling over one another,—too much confusion. This is not a large vessel yonder. We must have room on deck to swing and cut."

"I will have my men away in ten minutes, Lieutenant Maynard," crisply replied the blonde, raw-boned Scotsman with a finger at his hat-brim in courteous salute. He proceeded to call the men by name, strapping, sober fellows who had followed the sea amid the frequent perils of the merchant service. Jack Cockrell was the only landsman and he felt greatly honored that he should be included. Gone was his unmanly trepidation. Was he more worthy to live than these humble seamen who fought to make the ocean safer for other voyagers, who were true kinsmen of the Elizabethan heroes of blue water? He tarried a moment to wring Joe Hawkridge's hand in farewell and to tell him:

"If I have ill luck in this adventure, old comrade,—do you mind presenting my best compliments, and—and a fond farewell to Mistress Dorothy Stuart?"

"Strike me, Jack, stow that or you'll have me blubberin'," said Joe. "Bring me a lock of Cap'n Teach's whiskers as a token for my lass in Fayal if ever I clap eyes on her again. And you'd best take this heavy cutlass which I whetted a-purpose for ye. 'Twill split a pirate like slicin' an apple."

With this useful gift in his hand, Master Cockrell swung himself into the boat where Colonel Stuart stood in the stern-sheets. Perhaps he, too, was dwelling on a fair maid named Dorothy who might be left fatherless before the sun climbed an hour higher. The sloops were moving nearer the cay under sail and oar, trailing their crowded boats behind them. Blackbeard had hauled two or three of his guns into such positions that he could open fire but the sloops crawled doggedly into the shoal water and so screened their boats until these were ready to cast off for the final dash.

It was a rare sea picture, the stranded brig with canvas loose on the yards and ropes streaming, her listed decks a-swarm with pirates in outlandish, vari-colored garb, the surf playing about her in a bright dazzle and the gulls screaming overhead. The broad, squat figure of Blackbeard himself was never more conspicuous. He no longer strutted the quarter-deck but was all over the ship, menacing his men with his pistols, shifting them in groups for defense, shouldering bags of munitions, or heaping up the grenades and stink-pots to be lighted and thrown into the attacking boats.

It was his humor to adorn himself more elaborately than usual. Under his broad hat with the great feather in it he had stuck lengths of tow matches which were all sputtering and burning so that he ran to and fro in a cloud of sparks and smoke like that Evil One whom he professed to admire. He realized, no doubt, that this was likely to be his last stand. The inferno which he was so fond of counterfeiting, fairly yawned at his feet.

And now the sloops let go their anchors while from astern of them appeared the three boats of the assailants. They steered wide of each other to seek different parts of the pirate brig and so divide Blackbeard's force. The boats of Colonel Stuart and Lieutenant Maynard were racing for the honor of first place alongside. Blackbeard trained two guns on them, filled with grape and chain-shot, and one boat was shattered but it swam long enough for the cheering men to pull it to the brig and toss their grapples to the rail which was inclined quite close to the water. They were in the surf which broke against the ship, but this was a mere trifle.

Most of them went up the side like cats, leaping for the chains and dead-eyes, slashing at the nettings, swinging by a rope's end, or digging their toes in a crack of a gun-port. Forward they were pouring over the bowsprit, vaulting like acrobats from the anchor stocks, or swarming up the stays. It seemed beyond belief that they could gain footing on the decks with Blackbeard's demons stabbing and hacking and shooting at them, but in such manner as this was many a great sea fight won in the brave days of old.

Lieutenant Maynard gained his lodgment in the bows amid a swirl of pirates who tried to pen him in front of the forecastle house. But his tars of the Royal Navy were accustomed to close quarters and they straightway made room for themselves. Chest to chest and hand to hand they hewed their way toward the waist of the ship where Colonel Stuart raged like the braw, bonny Highlander that he was. Almost at the same time, the third boat had made fast under the jutting stern gallery and its twenty men were piling in through the cabin windows like so many human projectiles.

In the *King George* brigantine, Captain Jonathan Wellsby fidgeted and gnawed his lip, with a telescope at his eye, while he watched the conflict in which he could scarce distinguish friend from foe. He could see Blackbeard charge aft to rally his men and then whirl back to lunge into the mêlée where towered Colonel Stuart's tall figure. The powder smoke from pistols and muskets drifted in a thin blue haze. Joe Hawkridge was fairly shaking with nervousness as he said to the skipper:

"There'll be no clearing the decks 'less they down that monster of a Cap'n Teach. And he has more lives than a cat. See you my dear crony, Master Jack?"

"No, I cannot make him out in that mad turmoil," replied Captain Wellsby. "Nip and tuck, I call it, Joe."

This was the opinion forced upon Lieutenant Maynard as he saw the engagement resolve itself into a series of bloody whirlpools, his seamen and the pirates intermingled. He won his way past the forecastle into the wider spaces of the deck, with only a few of his twenty tars on their feet. Colonel Stuart was hard pressed and the boarders who had come over the stern had as much as they could do to hold their own. Thus far the issue was indecisive.

Jack Cockrell had kept close to the colonel, and felt amazement that he was still alive. His cheek was laid open, a bullet had torn his thigh, and a powder burn streaked his neck, but he felt these hurts not at all. It was a nightmare from which there seemed no escape. He saw Blackbeard rush at him with a raucous shout of:

"The scurvy young cockerel! He will ne'er crow again."

Colonel Stuart sprang between them, blades clashed, and they were swept apart in another wave of jostling combat. A moment later the colonel slipped and fell as a coal-black negro chopped at him with a broken cutlass. Jack Cockrell flew at him and they wrestled until a hip-lock threw the negro to the deck, where the colonel made him one pirate less.

Formidable as these outlaws were, they lacked the stern cohesion which had been drilled into the sailors of the Royal Navy and likewise learned in the hard school of the merchant service. Very slowly the odds were shifting against Blackbeard's crew. It was unmistakable when Lieutenant Maynard cut his way through to join Colonel Stuart, while the third group of boarders was advancing little by little from the after quarter. This meant that the force was gradually uniting in spite of the furious efforts to scatter it.

And now there came an episode which lives in history two centuries after that scene of carnage on the decks of the stranded brig. It has preserved the name of a humble lieutenant of the Royal Navy and saved it from the oblivion which is the common lot of most brave men who do and dare when duty beckons.

Blackbeard was bleeding from a dozen wounds and yet his activity was unabated. He was like a grizzly bear at bay. His men began to believe that his league with Satan, of which he obscenely boasted, had made him invulnerable. He was all that he had proclaimed himself to be, the wickedest and most fearsome pirate of the Western Ocean. And all the while, the slender, boyish Lieutenant Maynard, sailor and gentleman, had one aimin mind, and that was to slay Captain Edward Teach with his own hand. Nor was he at all content until he had cleared a path to where the hairy pirate was playing havoc with his broadsword.

With a loud laugh in mockery, Blackbeard snatched a loaded pistol from one of his men and fired at this foppish young officer who presumed to single him out. The ball chipped Maynard's ear and he dodged the pistol which was hurled at his head. It was curious to note a lull in the general engagement, a little interval of suspense while men regained their breath or tried to staunch their wounds. They were unconsciously awaiting the verdict of this duel between their leaders. Jack Cockrell, for instance, finding himself alone by some chance, leaned against a stanchion and heard his own blood drip—drip—on the deck.

It was a fleeting respite. Blackbeard swung his sword, with the might of those wide shoulders behind it. The lieutenant stepped aside like lightning and the bright weapon whistled past his arm. Then they went at each other like blacksmiths, sparks flying as steel bit steel. Dexterity and a cool wit were a match for the pirate's untamable strength. Gory, snarling, Blackbeard shortened his stroke to use the point. The lieutenant dropped to one knee, thrust upward, and found a vital spot.

Blackbeard stood staring at him with wonder in his eyes. Then those thick, bowed legs gave way and hetoppled like a tree uprooted. He passed out quietly enough, with no more cursing, and in this last moment of sensibility his thoughts appeared to wander far to his youth as a brisk merchant seaman out of Bristol port, for he was heard to mutter, with a long sigh:

"A pretty babe as ever was, Mollie, and the mortal image of its mother."

To his waist the sable beard covered him like a pall and one corded arm was flung across his breast and it showed the design of the skull and cross-bones pricked in India ink. Then as if the dead leader had issued the command, the surviving pirates began to fling down their weapons and loudly cry for quarter. They need not have felt ashamed of the resistance they had made up to this time, but now the delirium of combat had slackened and Blackbeard was no more. One or two of his officers were alive and they knew that the game was lost. Reinforcements could be sent from the sloops and the brigantine as soon as they were signaled for. And there was no flight from a stranded ship. Blackbeard had been able to infuse them with his own madness. Better chance the gallows than no quarter.

Here and there a few of the most desperate dogs of the Spanish Main who had followed Blackbeard's fortunes a long time, refused to surrender but they were either shot down or overpowered. Captain Wellsby was sending off two boats from the *King*

George with his surgeon, and the sloops were kedging in closer to thecay with the rising tide. Half the seamen were beyond aid and of the pirates no more than twenty were alive. Jack Cockrell was thankful to have come off so lightly, and he consoled himself with the notion that a scar across his cheek would be a manly memento. Colonel Stuart had been several times wounded but 'tis hard killing a Highlander.

It was Lieutenant Maynard's duty to offer public proof that he had slain none other than the infamous Blackbeard, wherefore he made no protest when his armorer hacked off the head of the dead pirate. There was no feeling of chivalry due a fallen foe, valiant though his end had been. This horrid trophy was tied at the end of a sloop's bowsprit, to be displayed for the gratification of all honest sailormen who might behold it in port. It was not a gentle age on blue water and Captain Edward Teach had been the death of many helpless people during his wicked career.

Lieutenant Maynard announced that he would take the two sloops into Bath Town, before proceeding to Virginia, as they were overcrowded vessels and the survivors of the boarding party needed proper care ashore. It would also afford the unscrupulous Governor Eden of North Carolina an opportunity to see his friend, Captain Teach, as a pirate who would divide no more plundered merchandise with him.

The brigantine *King George* was ready to escort them into Pamlico Sound, after which she would sail forCharles Town. Before the departure from the entrance of Cherokee Inlet, the stranded vessel was set afire and blazed grandly as the funeral pyre of Blackbeard's stout lads who would go no more a-roving.

Never was a nurse more devoted than Joe Hawkridge when his comrade was mercifully restored to him. Jack was woefully pale and weak but in blithe spirits and thankful to have seen the last of Blackbeard.

"Hulled in the leg and a damaged figger-head," said Joe, as he sat on the edge of the hero's bunk. "Triflin', I call it, when I expected to see you come aboard feet first wrapped in a bit o' canvas."

"I don't want to talk about it, Joe. Let's find something pleasant. Ho for Charles Town, and the green trees and a bench in the shade."

"And a tidy little vessel after a while, you and me and the Councilor a-pleasurin' up the coast with men and gear to fish up the treasure chest."

"And you believe that Blackbeard never got back to the Inlet to save the treasure for himself?" asked Jack.

"Not the way his ship was headed when she struck the shoal."

The brigantine was well on her way to Charles Town when Captain Wellsby found that Master Cockrell could be carried into the comfortable main cabin to rest on a cushioned settle for an hour or two at a time. It was during one of these visits, when Joe Hawkridge was present, that the skipper remembered to say

"Here is a bit of memorandum which may entertain you lads. Lieutenant Maynard had Blackbeard's quarters searched before the brig was burned. Some valuable stuff was found, but nothing what you'd call a pirate's treasure."

The lads looked at each other but kept their own counsel and Captain Wellsby went on to explain:

"There was a private log, Blackbeard's own journal, with a few entries in it, and most of the leaves torn out. I made a copy of what could be read, for the late Captain Teach was a better pirate than scrivener. Here, Jack, you are the scholar."

Jack read aloud this extract, which was about what might have been expected:

"Such a day! Rum all out,—our company somewhat sober. A confusion amongst us,—rogues a-plotting—great talk of separation. So I looked sharp for a prize. Took one, with a great deal of liquor on board, so kept the company hot, very hot. Then all things went well again."

"That sounds familiar enough to me," was Joe Hawkridge's comment. "And the rest of his writing will be much like it."

"Not so fast," exclaimed Captain Wellsby. "Scan the next page, Jack. 'Twill fetch you up all standing. Not that it puts gold in our pockets, for we know not where to search, but I swear it will make your eyes sparkle and your mouth waterTrying to hide his excitement, Jack saw a kind of rough inventory, and it ran like this:

"Where I Hid Itt This Cruse:

1 Bag 54 Silver Barrs. 1 Bag 79 Barrs & Peaces of Silver.

1 Bag Coyned Gold. 1 Bag Dust Gold. 2 Bags Gold Barrs.

1 Bag Silver Rings & Sundry Precious Stones. 3 Bags Unpolyshed Stones.

1 Silver Box set with Diamonds. 4 Golden Lockets.

Also 1 Silver Porringer—2 Gold Boxons—7 Green Stones—Rubies
Great & Small 67—P'cl Peaces of Eight & Dollars—Also 1 Bag
Lump Silver—a Small Chaine—a corral Necklace—1 Bag English
Crowns."

Captain Jonathan Wellsby listened to this luscious recital with an
air of mild amusement. He was of a temper too stolid and sensible
to waste his time on random treasure hunting. Blackbeard might
have chosen his hiding-place anywhere along hundreds of leagues
of coast. He could understand the agitation of these two
adventurous lads to whom this memorandum was like a magic
spell. Of such was the spirit of youth.

"Any more of it?" demanded Joe Hawkridge.

"The next page was ripped out of the journal," answered the
skipper. "What cruise did he mean? If it was this last one, he may
have hid it on the Virginia or Carolina coast

Master Cockrell gave it as an excuse that he had sat up long enough
and would return to his bunk. He was fairly bursting for a
conference with Joe, and as soon as they were alone he exclaimed:

"It may be the sea-chest! What do you think?"

"A handsome clue, I call it, something to warm the cockles of your
heart," grinned the sea urchin. "Aye, Jack, I should wager he wrote
that down whilst he lay at anchor in Cherokee Inlet."

"It seems shabby of us to keep the secret from Captain Wellsby,
but there is an obligation on us——"

"To Bill Saxby and the old sea wolf," said Joe. "We'll not forget this trump of a skipper when it comes to splittin' up the treasure."

"I am anxious for Captain Bonnet and his crew," remarked Jack. "With this crusade against pirates afoot, our friends may be hanged before we see them again."

CHAPTER XVIII

THE OLD BUCCANEER IS LOYAL

SORROW mingled with rejoicing when the *King George* brigantine sailed into Charles Town harbor. The sea fight off Cherokee Inlet had taken a heavy toll of brave seamen and there were vacant chairs and aching hearts ashore, but the fiendish Blackbeard had been blotted out and would no more harry the coast. Small and rude as was this pioneer settlement, it was most fair and attractive to the eyes of young Master Cockrell and Joe Hawkridge. In the house of Uncle Peter Forbes they rested at their ease and planned sedate careers for themselves.

Even the treasure ceased to be uppermost in their lively discussions. It could wait a while. They were no longer under the spell of its influence. This different world in which they now dwelt so contentedly made their adventures seem like shadowy figments with precious little romance in them. And neither lad expressed any great anxiety to go exploring the noisome Cherokee swamp and to challenge the ghost of Blackbeard.

Without a sign of rebellion, Jack returned to his books and lessons in Parson Throckmorton's garden. The learning already acquired he began to pass on to Joe Hawkridge, who was a zealous pupil and determined to read and write and cipher without letting the grass grow under his feet. It was this young pirate's ambition to make a shipping merchant of himself, and Councilor Forbes found him employment in a warehouse where the planters traded their rice, resin, and indigo for the varied merchandise brought out from England. Jack aspired to manage his uncle's plantation and to acquire lands of his own and some day to sit in the Governor's Council.

Of a Sunday morning he went to the little English church, dressed in his best and using a cane, for he limped from the wound in his thigh. Joe Hawkridge walked with him, careful to banish his grin, and sat in the Councilor's pew where he paid proper attention to the prayers and responses. This caused some gossip but the ocean waif was winning his way to favor by dint of industry, a shrewd wit, and his perennial good humor.

Frequently they escorted fair Dorothy Stuart home from church. She was fonder than ever of stalwart Master Cockrell because the colonel had told her he would have been a dead man had not the lad intervened to save him from the stroke of a negro pirate. Alas, however, it was not that sentimental devotion for which the lovelorn Jack yearned, and he confided to Joe that his existence was blighted. This evoked no sympathy from the fickle Hawkridge, who was forgetting his black-eyed lass in the Azores and was already a slave toDorothy Stuart. She laughed at them both and was their true friend, tender, and whimsical and anxious for their welfare. It was a valuable chapter in their education.

One morning while Joe was at work in the warehouse near the harbor, he heard a commotion in the street and was about to run out when his employer came in and explained:

"Two pirates captured,—just as I happened to pass. The knaves landed from a boat in broad daylight, unaware that Charles Town has mended its loose habit toward such gentry."

"What will be done with 'em?" quickly asked Joe, with an unhappy premonition.

"They were recognized as two of Stede Bonnet's old hands that used to resort to the tavern. Soldiers of the Governor's guard have been sent for to drag them to the gaol."

Joe hastened out but slackened his pace to lag behind the crowd of idlers who were jostling the prisoners along with hoots and jeers. Yes, there was the tall, gaunt frame and gray head of old Trimble Rogers whose mien was so forbidding and masterful that the mob forbore to handle him too roughly, unarmed though he was. At his elbow trudged chubby Bill Saxby, gazing about him with those wide blue eyes in which was not a trace of guile. Joe realized that for him to intercede would make matters worse. He was a reformed pirate onprobation and was known to have sailed with Blackbeard himself.

Therefore he darted into another street and sped to find Jack Cockrell, who chanced to be at home. They rushed into the room where Uncle Peter Forbes was writing at his desk and informed him that their two staunch comrades had come ashore to find them and were already in custody and something must be done to save them from the wrath of Governor Johnson, who had a mortal distaste for pirates still at large. The Councilor calmed the perturbation by assuring them:

"I have already spoken to His Excellency in behalf of these two men should they appear in this port. He was not wholly pleased but promised clemency should they offer to repent and if I gave surety for the pledge."

"They will be ready to live as respectable as Joe," impetuously declared Master Cockrell. "I'll go bail on it. Bill Saxby is a tradesman by nature and if you will lend him enough money to set himself up as a linen-draper and haberdasher, Uncle Peter, he can live happily ever after."

"And old Trimble Rogers has sailed his last cruise under the Jolly Roger, Councilor," put in Joe Hawkridge. "His timbers are full o' dry rot and he seeks a safe mooring."

"There seems no end to the bad company you drag me into," quoth Uncle Peter. "My hat and broadcloth cloak, Jack, and let us fare to the gaol and see whatthese awkward visitors have to say. After that I will attend upon the Governor."

In better spirits the anxious lads followed the dignified Secretary of the Council to the strongly built gaol on the edge of the town. In a very gloomy cell behind iron bars they found the luckless brace of pirates, shackled hand and foot. Bill Saxby took it like a placid philosopher but the ancient buccaneer was spitting Spanish oaths and condemning the hospitality of Charles Town in violent terms. He quieted instantly at sight of his young friends and the harsh, wrinkled visage fairly beamed as he shouted:

"Our *camaradas*, Bill. Here they be, to haul us out of this filthy hole! I forgive the unmannerly folks that allus used to welcome us."

They shook hands through the bars while Uncle Peter stood aside. He felt that his official station forbade his joining this fraternal reunion. In the narrow corridor he chatted with the gaoler to pass the time while Bill Saxby was explaining to the lads:

"We was in duty bound, in a manner of speakin', to run you down as soon as possible and make a report. Eh, Trimble?"

"Aye, Bill, to see what was to be done about the treasure. We wouldn't have 'em think we had run off with it. D'ye see, Master Cockrell, me and Bill took Cap'n Bonnet into our confidence. He is an honorable man and to be mentioned along with the great Cap'n Ed'ardDavis what I was shipmates with in the South Sea and at the sack of——"

"Stow it, grandsire," cried Bill. "I don't want to linger in gaol while you spin that long-winded yarn. Tell the lads what they want to know."

"If I weren't chained to the wall, Bill, I'd put my fist in your eye," severely retorted the veteran. "As I was a-sayin', Cap'n Bonnet was all courtesy and allowed the treasure belonged to us and he was ready to help find it."

"We told him we had to join up with our gentleman partner, Master Cockrell, and win his consent," said Bill, "afore we put our hooks on that blessed sea-chest."

"Which is exactly how I felt about you," Jack told them and he was greatly touched by this proof of their unbending fidelity. "But how did you manage it to reach Charles Town?"

"Cap'n Bonnet hove to outside the bar last night," explained Trimble Rogers, "and gave us a handy boat to sail in with."

The wary Joe Hawkridge took alarm at this and put a finger to his lips. It was unwise to parade the fact that Stede Bonnet cruised so near. His Excellency, the Governor, was anxious that he should share the fate of Blackbeard. Jack Cockrell had no fear that his Uncle Peter would be a tale-bearer. His private honor would forbid because this interview with the two lads was a privileged communication. What made Jack a trifle anxious was the presence of the gaol keeper in the corridor. He was a sneaking sort of man, soft of tread and oily of speech and inclined to curry favor with those in authority.

Councilor Peter Forbes had tactfully withdrawn this person beyond earshot but he began to edge toward the cell. Old Trimble Rogers tried to heed Joe's cautionary signal but what he meant to be a whisper was a hoarse rumble as he explained:

"Cap'n Bonnet sends word he will be off this coast again in thirty days. He will come ashore hisself, to Sullivan's Island to get the answer, whether you are to go with us, Master Cockrell, to Cherokee Inlet."

Jack glanced at the gaol keeper but he was a dozen feet away and deep in talk with Mr. Forbes. There was no sign that this confidence had been overheard. Bill Saxby scolded the buccaneer for his careless speech but the old man had been a freebooter too long to be easily tamed. With artful design, Jack led him away from this dangerous ground and suggested:

"You are done with pirating? And will you both be ready to stay ashore in Charles Town after this,—this certain errand is accomplished?"

"I swear it gladly and on my own Bible," answered Trimble Rogers.

"Swear it for me," said Bill Saxby.

Mr. Forbes interrupted and told the lads to go home and await his conference with Governor Johnson. It proved to be a session somewhat stormy but the upshotwas a pardon conditioned on good behavior. The convincing argument was that these men had been faithful to Master Cockrell through thick and thin and had saved him from perishing in the Cherokee swamp. Moreover, it might be an inducement to others of Stede Bonnet's crew to surrender themselves and forsake their evil ways.

No sooner were these two pirates released from gaol than they found an active friend in Mr. Peter Forbes. He went about it quietly, for obvious reasons, but he felt under great obligation to them for their goodness to his nephew. Just at this time one of the shop-keepers became a bankrupt because of unthrifty habits and too much card-playing. Through an agent, Peter Forbes purchased the stock of muslins and calicos, of brocades and taffetas, calash bonnets, satin petticoats, shoe-buckles, laces, and buttons. And having given his promissory notes for said merchandise, Bill Saxby proudly hung his own sign-board over the door.

There was a flutter among the ladies. Here was a noteworthy sensation, to be served by an obsequious pirate with innocent blue eyes who had sailed the Spanish Main. A few days and it was evident that William Saxby, late of London, would conduct a thriving trade. He was fairly enraptured with his good fortune and congenial occupation and took it most amiably when Jack Cockrell or Joe Hawkridge sauntered in to tease him. He was a disgrace to Stede Bonnet, said they, and never had a pirate fallen to such a low estate as thisTrimble Rogers was in no situation to rant at smug William, the linen draper. The old sea wolf who had outlived the most glorious era of the storied buccaneers, had a few gold pieces tucked away in his belt and at first he was content to loaf about the tavern, with an audience to listen to his wondrous tales which ranged from Henry Morgan to the great Captain Edward Davis. But he had never been a sot or an idler and soon he found himself lending a hand to assist the landlord in this way or that. And when disorder occurred, a word from this gray, hawk-eyed rover was enough to quell the wildest roisterers from the plantations.

Children strayed to the tavern green to sit upon his knee and twist those fierce mustachios of his, and their mothers ceased to snatch them away when they learned to know him better. Sometimes in his leisure hours he pored over his tattered little Bible with muttering lips and found pleasure in the Psalmist's denunciation of his enemies who were undoubtedly Spaniards in some other guise. He puttered about the flower beds with spade and rake and kept the bowling green clipped close with a keen sickle. In short, there was a niche for Trimble Rogers in his old age and he seemed well satisfied to fill it, just as Admiral Benbow spent his time among his posies at Deptford when he was not bombarding or blockading the French fleet off Dunkirk.

Jack Cockrell halted for a chat while passing the tavern and these two shipmates retired to a quiet cornerof the porch. The blind fiddler was plying a lively bow and a dozen boys and girls danced on the turf. Trimble Rogers surveyed them with a fatherly aspect as he said:

"They ain't afeard of me, Jack, not one of 'em. Was ever a worn out old hulk laid up in a fairer berth?"

"None of the sea fever left, Trimble? What about Captain Bonnet? He is due off the bar two days hence. My uncle frowns upon my sailing with him to seek the treasure. He insists that I steer clear of pirates."

"And that's entirely proper, Jack. I look at things different like, now I be a worthy citizen. 'Tis better to fit out a little expedition of our own, if we can drag silly Bill out of his rubbishy shop."

"Oh, he will come fast enough after a while. We are all tired of the sea just now," said Jack. "What about Captain Bonnet and meeting him at Sullivan's Island to pass the word that we must decline his courteous invitation?"

"I shall tend to that," answered the retired buccaneer, "And from what gossip I glean in the tavern, Cap'n Bonnet had best steer for his home port of Barbadoes and quit his fancy piratin'. This fractious Governor has set his heart on hangin' him. And Colonel Stuart is up and about again and has ordered the *King George* to fit for sea. 'Tis rumored he has sent messages to the north'ard for Lieutenant Maynard to sail another cruise in his company."

"Then be sure you warn Stede Bonnet," strongly advised Jack. "I would not be disloyal to the Province or to mine own good uncle, but one good turn deserves another."

Two days after this, Trimble Rogers vanished from the tavern and found Jack's canoe tied in a cove beyond the settled part of the town. It was in the evening of this same day that Jack was reading in his room by candle-light when a tap-tap on the window shutter startled him. He threw it open and dimly perceived that Dorothy Stuart stood there. Her face was white in the gloom and she wore a dress of some dark stuff. At her beckoning gesture, Jack slipped through the window and silently led her into the lane.

"Oh, Jack, I have been so torn betwixt scruples," she softly confided. "And I hope I am not doing wrong. If I am disloyal to my dear father, may I be forgiven. But I have made myself believe that there is a stronger obligation."

"It concerns Stede Bonnet," murmured Jack, reading the motive of this secret errand.

"Yes, you are bound to befriend him, Jack, on your honor as a gentleman."

"He has been warned to keep clear of Charles Town, Dorothy. Trimble Rogers has gone off to meet him."

"But it is worse than that. The keeper of the gaol, Jason Cutter, was closeted with my father this morning. I heard something that was said. Soldiers have been sent to Sullivan's Island

"To capture Captain Bonnet?" wrathfully exclaimed Jack. "Did Colonel Stuart go with them? Does he know why Stede Bonnet risks putting into this harbor in a small boat? It is to do a deed of pure friendship and chivalry."

"All my father understands is what the gaoler reported," replied Dorothy, "and the Governor acted on this evidence. No, he did not go with the troops but sent a major in command."

"Too late for me to be of service, alas! If they take Captain Bonnet alive, he will most certainly hang. And Bill Saxby and Trimble

Rogers will be embroiled in some desperate attempt to aid his escape from gaol."

"I am a dreadful, wicked girl to be thus in league with pirates," sighed Mistress Dorothy, "but I confess to you, Jack dear, that it would grieve my heart to see this charming pirate wear a hempen halter."

"My rival, is he? So I have found you out," flared Jack, pretending vast indignation. "Nevertheless, I shall still be true to him."

"And to me, I trust," she fondly replied. "Oh, I feel so thankful that faithful Trimble Rogers is keeping tryst. He will hear the soldiers blundering about in time to make Captain Bonnet take heed and shove off."

Jack walked home with her, very glad of the excuse, but with jealousy rankling in his bosom. It was not a lasting malady, however, and he had forgotten it next morning when he went early to the tavern to look for Trimble Rogers. There he found the major of the detachment at breakfast with an extraordinary story to tell. He had made a landing on Sullivan's Island after dark and deployed some of his men to patrol the beach that faced the ocean. The squad which remained with him had surprised a man lurking amongst the trees. Pursued and fired at, he had led them an infernal chase until they burst out upon the open beach. There they heard the sound of oars and voices in a boat which was making in for the shore. The hunted man raised his voice in one stentorian shout of:

"Pull out to sea, Cap'n Bonnet. And 'ware this coast. The soldiers are on my heels. Old Trimble Rogers sends a fare-ye-well."

The boat was wrenched about in a trice and moved away from the island, soon disappearing in the direction of the bar. The major's men had shot at it but without effect. When they had rushed to capture the fugitive who had shouted the warning, they found him prone upon the sand. There was not a scratch on him and yet he was quite dead. The prodigious exertion had broken his heart, ventured the major, and it had ceased to beat. His body would be prepared for Christian burial because of the esteem in which he was already held by many of the townspeople.

To Jack Cockrell and Joe Hawkridge it was sad news indeed but tender-hearted Bill Saxby mourned like one who had lost a parent. He closed the shop for a day and hung black ribbons on the knob. They agreed that the end had come for Trimble Rogers as he would have wished it, giving his life in loyal service to a friend and master. And perhaps it was better thus than for the creeping disabilities of old age to overtake him.

"He knew he was liable to pop off," said Bill, "with the rheumatism getting closer to his heart all the time. And he told me, did Trimble, that his share of the treasure was to go to the poor and needy of the town. Orphans and such was Trimble's weakness."

CHAPTER XIX

THE QUEST FOR PIRATES' GOLD

A SMALL sloop was making its leisurely way up the Carolina coast with a crew of a dozen men all told. The skipper was Captain Jonathan Wellsby who was taking this holiday cruise before sailing for England to command a fine new ship in the colonial trade. In the cabin were Jack Cockrell and Joe Hawkridge, Councilor Peter Arbuthnot Forbes, and that brisk young linen draper William Saxby. In the forecastle were trusty seamen who had sailed in the *Plymouth Adventure*. The sloop's destination was Cherokee Inlet and she was equipped with tackle and gear for a peculiar kind of fishing.

For once they made a voyage without fear of pirates. Safely the sloop passed in by the outlying cay where the charred bones of Blackbeard's brig were washed by the surf. An anchorage was found in the bight where the *Revenge* had tarried, close by the beach and the greensward of the pirates' old camp. After diligent preparation all hands manned a boat which pulled into the mouth of the sluggish creek. With axes to clear the entanglements and men enough to shove over the muddyshoals the boat was slowly forced up-stream and then into the smaller creek at the fork of the waters.

Uncle Peter Forbes was as gay as a truant schoolboy. This was the lark of a lifetime. The two lads, however, were uneasy and depressed. To them this sombre region was haunted, if not by ghosts then by memories as unhappy. They would not have been surprised to see Blackbeard skulking in the tall grass, his head bound in red calico, his pistols cocked to ambush them. And, alas, old Trimble Rogers was not along to protect them with his musket. He had lived and dreamed in expectation of this quest.

"We'll find no treasure, nary a penny of it," dolefully observed Joe Hawkridge who had actually begun to shiver.

"Of course we can find the sea-chest, you ninny," scolded Jack.

"Dead or alive, Cap'n Ed'ard Teach flew away with it afore now," was Joe's rejoinder. "He was a master one at black magic."

"Don't chatter like an idiot," spoke up Uncle Peter who was wildly brushing the mosquitoes from a sun-blistered nose. "My faith, I cannot understand how you lads got out of this swamp alive. It breeds all the plagues of Egypt."

They came to the tiny lagoon and rounded the bend beyond which the pirogue had capsized Blackbeard's cock-boat. There was nothing to indicate that any human being had visited this lonely spot since that sensational encounter. No trees had been cut down to serve as purchases for lifting the sea-chest from its oozy hiding-place. It was agreed that some traces would have remained if Blackbeard had been at work here before his death.

A camp was made upon the higher ground of the knoll and the party went about its task with skill and deliberation. Jointed sounding rods of iron were screwed together and the exact position of the spot determined from Jack Cockrell's chart and description. But neither he nor Joe Hawkridge could be coaxed into lending more active assistance. They were afraid of disturbing the bones of the drowned seaman who had fled from Blackbeard's bloody dirk. Jack had seen him go down and it was not a pleasant recollection.

And so these two heroes who had faced so many other perils without flinching were content to putter about half-heartedly and let the others exert themselves.

All one day they prodded and sounded but struck only sunken logs. What gave them more concern than this was the discovery that the slender rods, sharpened to a point, could be driven through one yielding stratum after another of muck and ooze. Through myriad years the decaying vegetable matter of this rank swamp had been accumulating in these layers of muck. There was no telling how deep down the weight of the sea-chest might have caused it to settleMr. Peter Forbes began to lose his youthful optimism and took four men to go and dig in the knoll while the others continued to search for the chest. The wooden cross still stood above the grave of Jesse Strawn and the long-leaf pines murmured his requiem. Having selected at random a place where he thought treasure ought to be, the worthy Councilor wielded a shovel until he perspired rivers.

"Confound it, Blackbeard must have left a scrap of paper somewhere to give us the proper instructions," he complained. "'Tis the custom of all proper pirates. Look at the trouble he has put us to."

"I helped search the cabin afore the brig was set afire," replied one of the seamen, "and all the writin' we found was in the bit of a book with the leaves tore out, same as Cap'n Wellsby made a fair copy of."

"That explains it," cried Uncle Peter. "I have no doubt the vile Blackbeard destroyed his private note of where he hid it, just to make the matter more difficult for us honest men."

This was plausible, but it failed to solve the riddle. A day or two of impatient digging and the portly Secretary of the Council was almost wrecked in mind and body, what with insects and heat, ague and fatigue. The ardor of his companions had likewise slackened. The boat's crew swore that the condemned sea-chest must have sunk all the way to China. Joe Hawkridge still argued that Blackbeard had whisked it away in a] cloud of smoke and brimstone. The unhappy Mr. Peter Forbes suggested:

"What say you, lads, to dropping down to the sloop for a respite from this accursed swamp? There we can take comfort and discuss what is to be done next."

Captain Jonathan Wellsby, who was a stubborn man, urged that they fish once more for the sunken chest before taking a rest, and this was agreed to. The sounding rods were plied with vigor and, at length, one of them drove against some solid object deep in the mud. It was more unyielding than a water-soaked log. The iron rod was lifted and rammed down with a thud which was like metal striking against metal. The explorers forgot the torments of the swamp. Uncle Peter Forbes was in no haste to flee the mosquitoes and the fever.

The sailors began to rig the spars and tackle as a derrick set up on the bank of the creek, with grapple hooks like huge tongs to swing out over the water and grope in the muddy depths. Absorbed in this fascinating task, they were startled beyond measure to hear the *thump, thump* of thole-pins sounding from somewhere below them in the swamp. It was no Indian pirogue. Only a ship's boat heavily manned could make that cadenced noise of oars. Bill Saxby bade the men be silent while he held a hand at his ear and harkened with taut attention. The mysterious boat, following the winding channel of the creek, was drawing nearer Voices could be heard, a rough command, a curse, a laugh.

"No honest men, I warrant," growled Captain Jonathan Wellsby, ready to take command by virtue of long habit. "Who else can they be but pirates, plague 'em. And they are betwixt us and the sea. All hands ashore and look to your arms. Lively now."

They were bewildered and taken all aback. In this holiday excursion after Blackbeard's treasure the party had reckoned only with dead or phantom pirates. There was some confusion, while Bill Saxby bawled at the seamen as addle-pated lubbers. Deserting their boat, they scrambled to cover in the tall grass while those busy with the derrick gear rushed to catch up muskets and powder-horns.

The strange boat was steadily forging up-stream and presently it was disclosed to view no more than a cable-length away. It was a pinnace filled with ruffianly fellows, more than a score of them. No merchant seamen these but brethren of the coast, freebooters who were gallows-ripe. Bill Saxby was quick to recognize two or three of them as old hands of Blackbeard's crew who must have deserted their leader in time to escape his fate. Presumably they had recruited others of their own stamp to go adventuring in the Cherokee swamp. They could have only one purpose. The very sight of them was enough to explain it. They were in quest of treasure like bloodhounds trailing a scent

Against such a force as this, discretion was the better part of valor. A ferocious yell burst from the pinnace and a flight of musket balls whistled over the heads of the fugitives who had so hastily abandoned their operations with the derrick and gear and the boat. Stout Bill Saxby and his comrades, finding concealment in the swamp, primed their muskets and let fly a volley at the pinnace which was an easy target. A pirate standing in the stern-sheets clapped a hand to his thigh and sat down abruptly. Another one let go his oar to dangle a bloody hand.

The pinnace drifted with the tide and stranded on a weedy shoal while the blue powder smoke hung over it like a fog. For the moment it was a demoralized crew of pirates, roaring all manner of threats but at a loss how to proceed. The other party took advantage of this delay to beat a rapid retreat along the path which led to the knoll where the camp was pitched. Upon this higher ground they might hope to defend themselves against a force which outnumbered them. They ran at top speed, bending low, hidden from observation, avoiding the pools and bogs.

The pirates were diverted from their hostile intentions as soon as they caught sight of the tall spars and tackle, and the boat with its sounding rods and other gear. With a great clamor they swarmed out of the pinnace and began to investigate. This gave the refugees on the knoll a little time to make their camp morecompact, to wield the shovels furiously and throw up intrenchments, to cut down trees for a barricade, to fill the water kegs, to prepare to withstand an assault or a siege.

The sun went down and the infatuated pirates were still exploring the creek, convinced that they could straightway lay hold of the treasure they had come to find. They kindled a fire on the bank and evidently intended to pass the night there. This mightily eased the minds of the toilers upon the knoll. Their predicament was still awkward in the extreme but the fear of sudden death had been lifted. And it seemed possible that these bothersome pirates might conclude to leave them alone.

It went sorely against the grain, however, to be driven away from the precious sea-chest when it was almost within their grasp, to have to scuttle from this crew of scurvy pirates. Jack Cockrell was for making a sortie by night, gustily declaiming to his companions:

"The sentries will be drunk or drowsy. I know these swine. A well-timed rush and we can cut 'em down and pistol the rest. Didn't they open fire on us from the pinnace?"

"Aye, Jack, and we'll fight to save our skins," said the cool-headed Captain Wellsby, "but 'tis a desperate business to attack yon cut-throats, even by night, and there will be men of us hurt and killed. Blackbeard's gold is not worth it

"Right sensibly put," declared Mr. Peter Forbes. "We had best spend this night in felling more trees and notching logs to pile them breast high. If these pirates find the sea-chest, they will leave us unmolested. If they fail to find it, they may conclude that we have already discovered the treasure. In that event, they will storm the knoll and give us no quarter."

"It would be rank folly to surrender," said stout Bill Saxby. "There be men in the pinnace who have no love for me nor for the two lads. 'Twas a shrewd suspicion of theirs that Blackbeard had played secret tricks in this Cherokee swamp, what with his excursions in that little cock-boat."

Keeping vigilant watch, they labored far into the night until the camp on the knoll was a hard nut to crack, with its surrounding ditch and palisade of logs behind which a man could lie and shoot. Now and then it might have been noted that Jack Cockrell and Joe Hawkridge conferred with their heads together as though something private were in the wind. As soon as they were relieved from duty, some time before the dawn, they stole very softly away from the knoll and groped along the path which led to the creek. Curiosity and the impetuous folly of youth impelled them to reconnoitre the pirates' bivouac.

"We may hear something worth listening to," whispered Jack, "and perhaps we can crawl close and steal some of their arms"None of that," chided young Hawkridge. "I am a man of goodly station in Charles Town and I would go back with a whole hide."

"You have grown too respectable," grumbled Jack. "Here is the chance for one last fling——"

His words stuck in his throat. A gurgle of horrified amazement and he tumbled headlong into the grass with a bare, sinewy arm wrapped around his neck. He fought to free himself but the breath was fairly choked out of him. Joe Hawkridge was desperately thrashing about in the swamp, gasping and snorting, his cries also smothered. In a twinkling they were captives, their arms tightly bound behind them, the stifling grip of their necks unrelaxed. Weakened almost to suffocation, the two lads could make no lively resistance. Jack uttered one feeble shout for help but subsided when those strong fingers tightened the clutch on his windpipe.

The assailants made no sound. Not a word was uttered. There were several of them, for the helpless prisoners were picked up bodily and lugged along by the head and the heels. They expected to be taken into the pirates' camp, believing they had been surprised and overpowered by an outlying sentry post. It was an old game, reflected Joe Hawkridge, to hold them alive as hostages. But he was vastly puzzled when these silent kidnappers, deftly picking their way in the darkness, took a direction which led them away from the bank of the creek. They had forsaken the trampled path and were proceeding through the trackless swamp whose pitfalls were avoided by a sort of sixth sense.

A mile of this laborious, uncanny progress and the bearers dumped their burdens and paused to rest. The two lads dizzily crawled to their feet and peered at the shadowy figures surrounding them. They heard a guttural exclamation and words exchanged in a strange, harsh tongue.

"Indians, blow me!" hoarsely whispered Joe, his throat sore and swollen.

"Comrade ahoy!" croaked Jack. "No pirates these, but Yemassees. Do they save us for the torture?"

"God knows. 'Tis a sorry mischance as ever was. I'd sooner meet up with Blackbeard's ghost. Are ye badly hurt?"

"Like a man hanged by the neck, Joe, but no mortal wounds. Had we minded Uncle Peter we would be safe in the sloop by now. One more day of hunting that filthy treasure undid us."

The half dozen Yemassees squatted about them, talking in low tones, and offered no further violence. Presumably they were waiting for daybreak, having conveyed their prisoners beyond all chance of rescue. The two lads shivered with fear and weariness. They were bruised and breathless and the thongs which tightly bound their wrists made their arms ache intolerably. Bitter was the regret at invading this baleful Cherokeeswamp when they might have remained safe from all harm in pleasant Charles Town.

Sadly they watched the eastern sky grow brighter while the gloom of the desolate swamp turned wan and gray. The Indian captors became visible, brown, half-naked men wearing leggings and breech-clouts of tanned deerskin. Two of them carried muskets. They were not made hideous by war-paint, as Jack Cockrell was quick to note. He said to his companion:

"A hunting party, Joe. They were spying on our camp, like enough, or keeping watch of the pirates. No doubt they wonder why white men come to fight one another in the swamp."

"They will wish to find out from us," was the hopeful reply. "They seem a deal more curious than bloodthirsty. A stout heart, say I, and we may weather it yet."

Soon the lads were roughly prodded ahead and went stumbling and splashing through the marshy verdure and slippery ooze until they came to higher ground and easier walking. Upon this ridge they descried the camp of the Yemassees—huts fashioned of poles and bark and boughs, a freshly killed deer hanging from a tree, smoke rising from beneath a huge iron kettle, plump, naked children scampering in play with several barking dogs, the squaws shrilly scolding them. Several warriors lazily emerged from the huts, yawning, brushing the long black hair from their eyes

They moved more actively at perceiving the procession which approached from the swamp. Two or three ran back to the largest shelter and presently a big-bodied, middle-aged man strode out, his mien stern and dignified, his rank denoted by the elaborate fringed tunic of buckskin and the head-dress of heron plumes. He shouted something in a sonorous voice. The hunting party hastened forward, dragging the two English lads by the elbows and flinging them down at the feet of the chief. He stood with arms folded across his chest, scowling, formidable.

Then he spoke a few words of broken English, to the astonishment of the captives. He mentioned the names of settlements on the Cape Fear River where, it was inferred, he had been on friendly terms with the colonists. His manner was not so much hostile as questioning. In Charles Town both Joe and Jack had learned the common phrases of the Indian tongue such as were used among the merchants and traders. Pieced out with signs and gestures, they were able to carry on a halting dialogue with the chief of this small band.

They were able to comprehend that he hated pirates above all other men. He recognized the name of Blackbeard and indicated his great joy that this eminent scoundrel had met his just deserts. Many times the freebooters of the coast had hunted and slain the Indians for wanton sport. And perhaps the word had sped of that expedition of Captain Stede Bonnet out of CharlesTown when he had exterminated the Yemassees who had set out to harry and burn the near-by plantations. The two uneasy lads felt that they still stood in the shadow of death unless they could persuade the chief that they were not pirates, that they were in no way to be confused with the crew of blackguards which had ascended the creek in the pinnace.

The chief delayed his judgment. Two young men lifted the huge kettle from the fire. It was steaming with a savory smell of stewed meat. The captives were invited to join the others in spearing bits of venison with sharpened sticks. Chewing lustily, with a noble appetite, Joe Hawkridge confided:

"My spirits rise, Jack. An empty belly always did make a coward of me. How now, my lusty cockerel? Shall we flap our wings and crow?"

"Crow we must, or have our necks wrung as pirates," said Jack, gnawing a bone. "Which one of us shall make the first oration?"

"The nephew of the Councilor, of course," cried Joe, "with his cargo of Greek and Latin education. Make a power of noise, Jack."

And now indeed did young Master Cockrell prove that all those drudging hours with snuffy Parson Throckmorton had not been wasted. Standing in an open space, clear of the crowd, he addressed the chief in loud and impressive language. The gist of it was that he and his friends were the sworn foes of all piratesand especially anxious to rid the world of such vermin as those that had come into the Cherokee swamp in the great ship's boat and were encamped on the bank of the creek.

This other peaceful party entrenched on the knoll were honest, law-abiding men of Charles Town who would harm no one. They had come in search of pirates' gold. If the chief of the Yemassees would join forces with them and smoke the pipe of peace, they would drive those foul pirates out of the Cherokee swamp. And should the gold be found, it would be fairly divided between the godly men of Charles Town and their Indian allies. To bind this bargain Master Cockrell and Master Hawkridge were ready to pledge their honor and their lives.

It was a most eloquent effort delivered with much gesticulation. The Yemassee braves set in a circle and grunted approval. They liked the sound and fury of it. Jack hurled scraps of Homer and Virgil at them when at a loss for resounding periods. The chief nodded his understanding of such words as *pirates* and *gold* and actually smiled when Jack's pantomime depicted the death of Blackbeard on the deck of his ship. *Gold* was a magic word to these Indians. It would purchase muskets and powder and ball, cloth and ironmongery and strong liquors from the white men of the settlements.

The chief discussed it with his followers. Duringthe lull Joe Hawkridge said, with a long sigh of relief:

"My scalp itches not so much, Jack. The notion of having it twisted off with a dull blade vexed me. Ye did wondrous well. The mouth of Secretary Peter Forbes would ha' gaped wide open."

"Much sound and little sense, Joe, but methinks it hit the target. I took care to sprinkle it with such words as yonder savage could bite on."

"If we find no gold, the fat may be in the fire again, but it gives us time to draw breath."

They rubbed their chafed wrists and sat on the ground while the savages held a long pow-wow. The chief was explaining the purport of Master Cockrell's impressive declamation. There was no enmity in the glances aimed at the English lads. It was more a matter of deliberation, of passing judgment on the truth or the falsity of the story. It was plain to read that the Yemassees desired to lay greedy hold of Blackbeard's gold. They were like children listening to a fairy tale. The fat little papooses crawled timidly near to inspect the mysterious strangers and scrambled away squealing with delicious terror.

The hours passed and the verdict was delayed. Two young braves stole away into the pine woodland on some errand, at the behest of the chief. It was after noon when they returned. With them came a dozen Yemassee warriors from another hunting camp, strong] quick-footed men in light marching order who were armed with long bows and knives. The chief spoke a few words and mustered his force. All told he had more than thirty picked followers. The English lads were told to move with them.

In single file the band flitted silently along the ridge and plunged into the swamp. The prisoners were closely guarded. At the slightest sign of treachery the long knives would slither between their ribs. This they well knew and their devout prayer was that their friends on the knoll might not commit some rash act of hostility and so ruin the enterprise. With heart-quaking trepidation they perceived at some distance the rude barricade of logs and the yellow streaks of earth hastily thrown up.

The cautious Yemassees concealed themselves as though the swamp had swallowed them up. The chief made certain signs, and the lads understood his meaning. Jack Cockrell ripped a sleeve from his shirt and tied it to a stick as a flag of truce. Joe Hawkridge advanced with them, the stalwart chief between them, his empty hands extended in token of peace. The ambushed Yemassees, lying in the tall grass, were ready to let fly with musket balls and flights of arrows or to storm the knoll.

A sailor on sentry duty gave the alarm and the lads saw a row of heads bob above the logs, and the gleam of weapons. Then Captain Jonathan Wellsby movedout into the open and was joined by Mr. Peter Forbes. They stood gazing at the singular spectacle, the bedraggled runaways who had vanished without trace, the odd flag of truce, the brawny, dignified savage making signs of friendship. The men in the stockade were ordered to lay down their arms. They came running out to cheer and wave their hats.

Mr. Peter Forbes was torn betwixt affection and the desire to scold his flighty nephew. They met half-way down the slope and Jack hastened to explain:

"Before you clap us in irons as deserters, Uncle Peter, grant a parley, if you please. Our lives hang by a hair."

"God bless me, boy, we thought the pirates had slain you both," spluttered Uncle Peter, a tear in his eye. "What means this tall savage?"

"A noble chief of the Yemassees who used us with all courtesy," said Jack.

Captain Wellsby had drawn Joe Hawkridge aside and was swiftly enlightened concerning the alliance with the Indians. Presently they were holding a conference, all seated together in the shade of a tree. A tobacco pipe of clay, with a long reed for a stem, was lighted and passed from hand to hand. The chief puffed solemnly with an occasional nod and a grunt. It was agreed, with due ceremony, that the pirates should be attacked in their camp and driven away. The Yemassee warriors would make common cause with the Englishmen. As a reward, Blackbeard's treasure was to be fairly divided, half and half.

The chief raised his voice in a long, deep shout of summons and his band of fighting men emerged from their ambush in the swamp. There was no reason for delaying the movement against the pirates. The Yemassees were eager for the fray. They were about to advance through the swamp, cunningly hidden, while the Englishmen followed at a slower pace to spread out on the flanks. Just then there was heard a sudden and riotous commotion among the pirates at the creek. It was a mad, jubilant uproar as though some frenzy had seized them all. Bill Saxby leaned on his musket and listened for a long moment.

"The rogues have fished up the sea-chest, by the din they make," said he. "We left that sounding rod a-stickin' in the mud. They save us the trouble, eh, Captain Wellsby?"

The skipper laughed in his beard and floundered ahead like a bear. Jack Cockrell passed the word to the chief that the gold was awaiting them. Like shadows the Yemassees drew near the creek and then, full-lunged, terrific, their war-whoop echoed through the dismal Cherokee swamp. Nimble Jack Cockrell was not far behind them, his heart pumping as though it would burst.

He was in time to see four lusty pirates swaying at a rope which led through the pulley-blocks of the sparsthat overhung the creek as a tall derrick. They were hoisting away with all their might while there slowly rose in air a mud-covered, befouled sea-chest all hung with weeds and slimy refuse. Two other pirates tailed on to a guy rope and the heavy chest swung toward the bank, suspended in air.

At this moment the screeching chorus of the Indian war-whoop smote their affrighted ears, followed by the discharge of muskets. These startled pirates let go the tackle and the guy rope and, with one accord, leaped for the pinnace which floated close to the bank. The weighty sea-chest swinging in air came down by the run as the ropes smoked through the blocks. It had been swayed in far enough so that it fell not in the water but upon the edge of the shore between the derrick spars. The rusty hinges and straps were burst asunder as the treasure chest crashed upon a log and cracked open like an egg.

Out spilled a stream of doubloons and pieces of eight, a cascade of gold and silver bars, of jewels flowing from the rotten bags which had contained them. In this extraordinary manner was the hoard of the departed Blackbeard brought to light. The unfortunate pirates who had found the spoils tarried not to gloat and rejoice. They appeared to have urgent business elsewhere. In hot pursuit came the ravening Yemassees, yelling like fiends, assisted by the reinforcements of Captain Jonathan Wellsby

What saved the lives of these panic-smitten pirates was the dramatic explosion of that great treasure chest when it fell and smashed upon the log. Indians and Englishmen alike forgot their intent to shoot and slaughter. They rushed to surround the bewitching booty, to cut capers like excited urchins.

"Share and share," roared Captain Wellsby, shoving them headlong. "Half to the Yemassees and half to us. Our word is given. Stand back, ye lunatics, while we do the thing with order and decency."

Already the pinnace was filled with cursing pirates who saw that the game was lost. Some of them had left their weapons in camp, others fired a few wild shots, but those who had any wit left were tugging at the oars to make for the open sea.

"After 'em," roared Bill Saxby. "Follow down the creek to make sure they do not molest our sloop."

A score of men, Indians included, jumped into the boat and pulled in chase, no longer on slaughter bent. The only thought in their heads was to despatch the errand and return to squat around the treasure chest. Jack Cockrell and Joe Hawkridge remained to help scoop up the coin and jewels and stow them in stout kegs and sacks. The stoical chief of the Yemassees was grinning from ear to ear as he grunted:

"Plenty gold. Good! Hurrah, boys!"

Arm-in-arm Jack Cockrell and Joe Hawkridge danced a sailor's hornpipe upon the splintered lid of Blackbeard's sea-chest while they sang with all their might:

"For his work he's never loth,
An' a-pleasurin' he'll go,
Tho' certain sure to be popt off,
Yo, ho, with the rum below."

End of the book.

www.ingramcontent.com/pod-product-compliance
Lightning Source LLC
Chambersburg PA
CBHW072357290526
45794CB00001B/95